# AAT

**Indirect Tax**
Level 3
**Course Book**
For assessments from
1 January to 31 December 2017

First edition August 2016

ISBN 9781 4727 4815 7
ISBN (for internal use only) 9781 4727 4871 3

**British Library Cataloguing-in-Publication Data**
A catalogue record for this book is available from the British Library

**Published by**

BPP Learning Media Ltd
BPP House, Aldine Place
142-144 Uxbridge Road
London W12 8AA

www.bpp.com/learningmedia

Printed in the United Kingdom by Wheatons Exeter Ltd
Hennock Road
Marsh Barton
Exeter
EX2 8RP

BPP
LEARNING MEDIA

# Contents

# Introduction to the course

## Syllabus overview

This unit teaches students the knowledge and skills to calculate VAT and submit the VAT return. It involves extracting the relevant information from an organisation's accounting records; calculating the amount of VAT payable or reclaimable and resolving errors or omissions.

Students will also be able to submit completed documentation in a timely manner whilst maintaining an effective working relationship with the relevant tax authority.

### Test specification for this unit assessment

| Assessment method | Marking type | Duration of assessment |
|---|---|---|
| Computer based assessment | Partially computer / partially human marked | 1.5 hours |

## Assessment structure

1½ hours duration

Competency is 70%

*Note that this is only a guideline as to what might come up. The format and content of each task may vary from what we have listed below.

Your AQ16 assessment will consist of 8 tasks

| Task | Expected content | Max marks | Chapter ref | Study complete |
|------|------------------|-----------|-------------|----------------|
| Task 1 | Finding out about VAT, and registration | 6 | VAT basics, Accounting for VAT | |
| Task 2 | VAT invoices, tax point, making exempt supplies | 9 | Accounting for VAT, Inputs and outputs | |
| Task 3 | VAT schemes, due dates, bad debt relief | 5 | VAT schemes for small businesses, The VAT return | |
| Task 4 | Detailed VAT rules, corrections, ethics | 9 | Accounting for VAT, Administration | |
| Task 5 | VAT calculations and reconciliations | 7 | Inputs and outputs, The VAT return | |
| Task 6 | Preparing specific figures for the VAT return, corrections, ethics | 7 | The VAT return, Administration | |
| Task 7 | Completing and submitting a VAT return accurately | 17 | The VAT return | |
| Task 8 | Communicating VAT information | 10 | Administration | |

# Skills bank

Our experience of preparing students for this type of assessment suggests that to obtain competency, you will need to develop a number of key skills.

## What do I need to know to do well in the assessment?

*Indirect Tax* is designed to develop your skills in preparing and submitting returns to the relevant tax authority in situations where the transactions that have to be included are relatively routine.

To be successful in the assessment you need to:

- Understand and apply VAT legislation requirements

- Accurately complete VAT returns and submit them in a timely manner

- Understand the implications for the business of errors, omissions, and late filing and payment

- Report VAT-related information within the organisation in accordance with regulatory and organisational requirement

## Assumed knowledge

There is no assumed knowledge for this unit.

## Assessment style

In the assessment you will complete tasks by:

1   Entering narrative by selecting from drop down menus of narrative options known as **picklists**

2   Using **drag and drop** menus to enter narrative

3   Typing in numbers, known as **gapfill** entry

4   Entering **ticks**

5   Entering **dates** by selecting from a calendar

You must familiarise yourself with the style of the online questions and the AAT software before taking the assessment. As part of your revision, login to the **AAT website** and attempt their **online practice assessments**.

## Introduction to the assessment

The question practice you do will prepare you for the format of tasks you will see in the *Indirect Tax* assessment. It is also useful to familiarise yourself with the introductory information you may be given at the start of the assessment. For example:

You have 1 hour and 30 minutes to complete this assessment.

You should attempt and aim to complete EVERY task.

Each task is independent. You will not need to refer to your answers to previous tasks.

Read every task carefully to make sure you understand what is required.

Where the date is relevant, it is given in the task data.

Both minus signs and brackets can be used to indicate negative numbers UNLESS task instructions state otherwise.

The standard rate of VAT is 20%

You must use a full stop to indicate a decimal point.

For example, write 100.57 NOT 100,57 OR 100 57.

You may use a comma to indicate a number in the thousands, but you don't have to. For example, 10000 and 10,000 are both OK.

Other indicators are not compatible with the computer-marked system.

Reference data is provided in this assessment. The data has been broken down into sections to make it easier to search. You can access the data at any point by clicking on the section subject listed in the toolbar at the top right of every task.

When you click on a subject, the data will appear in a pop-up window. You can then move or close the window. When you move on to a new task, you will have to re-open a window to see the data again.

1   As you revise, use the **BPP Passcards** to consolidate your knowledge. They are a pocket-sized revision tool, perfect for packing in that last-minute revision.

2   Attempt as many tasks as possible in the **Question Bank**. There are plenty of assessment-style tasks which are excellent preparation for the real assessment.

3   Always **check** through your own answers as you will in the real assessment, before looking at the solutions in the back of the Question Bank.

## Key to icons

| | | |
|---|---|---|
| | **Key term** | A key definition which is important to be aware of for the assessment |
| | **Formula to learn** | A formula you will need to learn as it will not be provided in the assessment |
| | **Formula provided** | A formula which is provided within the assessment and generally available as a pop-up on screen |
| | **Activity** | An example which allows you to apply your knowledge to the technique covered in the Course Book. The solution is provided at the end of the chapter |
| | **Illustration** | A worked example which can be used to review and see how an assessment question could be answered |
| | **Assessment focus point** | A high priority point for the assessment |
| | **Open book reference** | Where use of an open book will be allowed for the assessment |
| | **Real life examples** | A practical real life scenario |

## Supplements

From time to time we may need to publish supplementary materials to one of our titles. This can be for a variety of reasons, from a small change in the AAT unit guidance to new legislation coming into effect between editions.

**You should check our supplements page regularly** for anything that may affect your learning materials. All supplements are available free of charge on our supplements page on our website at:

www.bpp.com/learning-media/about/students

## Improving material and removing errors

There is a constant need to update and enhance our study materials in line with both regulatory changes and new insights into the assessments.

From our team of authors BPP appoints a subject expert to update and improve these materials for each new edition.

Their updated draft is subsequently technically checked by another author and from time to time non-technically checked by a proof reader.

We are very keen to remove as many numerical errors and narrative typos as we can but given the volume of detailed information being changed in a short space of time we know that a few errors will sometimes get through our net.

We apologise in advance for any inconvenience that an error might cause. We continue to look for new ways to improve these study materials and would welcome your suggestions. Please feel free to contact our AAT Head of Programme at nisarahmed@bpp.com if you have any suggestions for us.

# Introduction to VAT

1

## Learning outcomes

Having studied this chapter you will be able to:

| 1.2 | Identify |
|-----|----------|
| | • That VAT is a tax on consumer spending, including knowing whether the tax falls on registered businesses or the end user |
| | • The relevant tax authority |
| **2.2** | Explain the basic principles of VAT |
| | • Know what are inputs and outputs |
| | • Know what is meant by input and output tax |

## Assessment context

An awareness of how the VAT system works within the UK.

Includes important terminology which is used throughout the course.

## Qualification and Business context

It is the responsibility of the business to collect VAT on behalf of HMRC. As an accountant, you should be aware of how this process works.

# Chapter overview

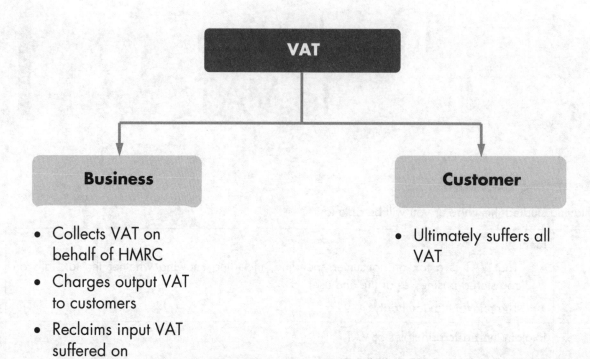

**VAT**

**Business**

- Collects VAT on behalf of HMRC
- Charges output VAT to customers
- Reclaims input VAT suffered on purchases

**Customer**

- Ultimately suffers all VAT

# Introduction

Value Added Tax (VAT) is an indirect tax which is essentially a sales tax – it is a tax on consumer expenditure and is an important source of revenue for the government. The basic principle is that VAT should normally be borne by the final consumer but is collected at each stage of the value added process.

---

**Key terms**

A VAT-registered trader will:

- Collect VAT by charging their customers VAT – **output VAT**
- Reclaim VAT they have suffered on their purchases – **input VAT**

---

Complete a VAT return which states how much VAT is payable to HMRC. The amount payable is the difference between the output VAT and the input VAT. HMRC (Her Majesty's Revenue and Customs) is the government department charged with the administration and collection of taxes.

The current rate of VAT is **20%**.

# 1 Role of a business

The business that is registered for VAT acts as an agent for HMRC, collecting VAT on their behalf. If the business adds value, it will owe output VAT to HMRC and that makes VAT a liability in the books of the business.

Businesses have to make sure they account for VAT accurately; otherwise they could face penalties.

# 2 Collection of VAT

It is the end consumer (normally the general public) who suffers the full amount of VAT. However, the VAT is collected by HMRC at each value added stage of the production process.

## Illustration 1: Collection of VAT

| | Net Sale Price £ | Net Purchase Price £ | VAT (@20%) £ |
|---|---|---|---|
| Producer sells raw materials for £100.00 + VAT | 100.00 | | 20.00 |
| Total payable by producer to HMRC | | | 20.00 |
| Factory buys the raw materials to manufacture their product. They then sell this product to a retailer for £300.00 + VAT | 300.00 | (100.00) | (20.00) |
| | | | 60.00 |
| Total payable by factory to HMRC | | | 40.00 |
| Retailer buys the product and sells it on to the end customer for £360.00 + VAT | | (300.00) | (60.00) |
| | 360.00 | | 72.00 |
| Total payable by retailer to HMRC | | | 12.00 |

| VAT paid to HMRC at each stage of the value added process is: | £ |
|---|---|
| Producer | 20.00 |
| Factory | 40.00 |
| Retailer | 12.00 |
| Total | 72.00 |
| | |
| **VAT suffered by end customer (who cannot reclaim) is:** | 72.00 |

## Activity 1: Input and output tax

Business A sells goods to Business B for £1,000 plus £200 of VAT.

**Required**

**Which business treats the VAT as input tax and which treats it as output tax?**

|  | Input tax ✓ | Output tax ✓ |
|---|---|---|
| Business A |  |  |
| Business B |  |  |

## Chapter summary

- VAT is an indirect tax administered by HM Revenue & Customs.
- A purchaser who is not VAT-registered bears the cost of the VAT. This is normally the final purchaser in the supply chain who is often a member of the public.

## Keywords

- **Input VAT or input tax:** VAT on the purchases of goods and payment of expenses. This is reclaimed by the business from HMRC.

- **Output VAT or output tax:** VAT on the sale of goods and the provision of services. This is paid by the business to HMRC.

## Activity 1: Input and output tax

|  | Input tax ✓ | Output tax ✓ |
|---|---|---|
| Business A |  | ✓ |
| Business B | ✓ |  |

## Test your learning

1   **Which organisation administers VAT in the UK? Tick the relevant box below.**

|  | ✓ |
|---|---|
| HM Customs & Excise | |
| Inland Revenue | |
| HM Revenue & Customs | |
| HM Treasury | |

2   **Choose which ONE of the following statements is correct. Tick the relevant box below.**

|  | ✓ |
|---|---|
| Output VAT is the VAT charged by a supplier on the sales that are made by his business. Output VAT is collected by the supplier and paid over to HMRC. | |
| Output VAT is the VAT suffered by the purchaser of the goods which will be reclaimed from HMRC if the purchaser is VAT-registered. | |

3   **Explain how it is normally the final consumer that pays the full amount of VAT to the seller but never pays any money to HMRC.**

# VAT basics

2

## Learning outcomes

Having studied this chapter you will be able to:

| 1.3 | Describe the VAT registration and deregistration requirements |
|---|---|
| | • Registering for VAT |
| | • Registration and deregistration thresholds for the normal VAT scheme, and how to apply them |
| | • The circumstances in which voluntary registration may be beneficial to the business |
| | • The deregistration threshold and circumstances in which deregistration may be appropriate |
| | • What is meant by the past turnover measure and the future turnover method, and how to comply with them in respect of registration |
| 2.2 | Identify the specific calculations needed for standard, reduced-rate, zero-rated and exempt supplies |
| | • Recognise the different implications of exempt supplies and of zero-rated supplies for the VAT return, and the effect on recovery of input tax |

## Assessment context

Task 1 in the exam may ask you to identify when a taxable trader needs to register for VAT and also what the impact of this will be on the business.

Task 2 in the exam may ask you about exempt supplies and the difference between a zero-rated supplier and an exempt supplier. There is no knowledge required of the detail of which specific items fall into each category of supply.

## Qualification context

Understand that not all businesses will need to be VAT-registered. However, if they are registered, you will need to know what the impact of this is.

## Business context

You will need to have an awareness that there are different rates of VAT for different types of product.

The benefits of registering for VAT are abundant to a business, but consideration must be given to potential drawbacks.

# Chapter overview

**VAT Basics**

**Scope of VAT**

**Registration**

**Taxable Supplies**

- 20%, 5% or 0%
- Can recover input VAT

**Exempt Supplies**

- No VAT impact
- Cannot recover input VAT

**Compulsory**

- Past turnover
- Future turnover
- Deregistration criteria

**Voluntary**

- Advantages and disadvantages

# 1 Scope of VAT

VAT is chargeable on **taxable supplies** of goods and services made in the UK by **taxable persons** in the course of their business.

A **taxable person** is an individual or company who is required to register for VAT, (see registration below).

**Taxable supplies** are those which are either:

- **standard-rated** (20%),

- **zero-rated** (0%) for example non-luxury food, children's clothing

- or **reduced-rated** (5%) for example domestic fuel.

**Exempt supplies** (for example insurance or postal services) are not taxable supplies. You will be told in the exam if a supply is taxable and if so, at which rate.

A supplier making solely taxable supplies may, or in certain circumstances must, register for VAT and can then recover the input VAT suffered on their purchases.

If a supplier only makes exempt supplies, then they cannot register for VAT and will not be able to recover input VAT suffered on their purchases.

## Illustration 1: Calculation of VAT Payable

|  | Type of supplies | | |
| --- | --- | --- | --- |
|  | Standard-Rated £ | Zero-Rated £ | Exempt £ |
| Supplies (net) | 30,000 | 30,000 | 30,000 |
| VAT charged on supplies | 6,000 | 0 | – |
|  | 36,000 | 30,000 | 30,000 |
| Purchases (net) | 20,000 | 20,000 | 20,000 |
| VAT charged on purchases (all purchases are standard-rated) | 4,000 | 4,000 | 4,000 |
|  | 24,000 | 24,000 | 24,000 |
| VAT payable/(reclaimable) | £2,000 | £(4,000) | Nil |

## 1.1 Cost to the business

- As businesses making taxable supplies which are registered for VAT can reclaim the input VAT paid on their purchases and expenses, the cost to the business is the VAT-exclusive amount.

- As businesses making only exempt supplies cannot register for VAT and therefore cannot reclaim the input VAT paid on their purchases and expenses, the cost to the business is the VAT-inclusive amount.

## Activity 1: Cost to business

The following businesses have just paid telephone bills of £1,200 (£1,000 plus VAT of £200).

**Required**

**What is the net cost incurred by each business in relation to the telephone bills?**

| Business type | Type of supply made | Net cost £ |
| --- | --- | --- |
| Insurance company | Only exempt supplies | |
| Accountancy firm | Only standard-rated supplies | |
| Bus company | Only zero-rated supplies | |

# 2 Registration

## 2.1 Compulsory registration

**Registration** is compulsory if a taxable person meets one of the following two tests:

**1  Past turnover ("Historic Test")**

Check at the end of each month if the total taxable turnover over the previous 12 months exceeds the registration limit of £83,000.

For a new business the period may be shorter, ie from the start of trade to the current month end. It must not, however, exceed 12 months.

**2  Future Test**

Each day check if the total taxable turnover over for just the next 30 days is likely to exceed the registration limit of £83,000.

**Taxable turnover** is the VAT exclusive value of all zero-rated, reduced-rated and standard-rated supplies.

If either test is passed, the taxable person must notify HMRC within 30 days of the date of the historic test; and without delay, for the future test.

Registration is effective from:

(a) Start of month following the end of the 30 day notification period (historic test)
(b) Start of 30 day period (future test)

### Illustration 2: Historic test

Jack started his business on 1 July 2016. His monthly VAT-exclusive turnover is:

| | £ |
|---|---|
| Standard-rated supplies | 7,000 |
| Zero-rated supplies | 2,850 |
| Exempt supplies | 600 |
| TOTAL | 10,450 |

1 Calculate the VAT exclusive **taxable turnover** for each month (standard plus zero-rated supplies). Exclude the exempt supplies.

 Taxable turnover is £9,850 per month (£7,000 + £2,850)

2 Work out when the £83,000 registration limit is exceeded (if at all), up to a maximum of a 12 month period.

 After eight months (28 February 2017) cumulative turnover is £78,800, so the limit is not exceeded.

 After nine months (31 March 2017) cumulative turnover is £88,650 so the limit is exceeded.

 Therefore after nine months, Jack must register for VAT within 30 days (ie by 30 April 2017). His registration will be effective from 1 May 2017.

### Illustration 3: Future test

Orla has been in business for many years with VAT-exclusive turnover of approximately £6,500 per month (£78,000 per annum) and so has not yet had to register under the historic test. On 24 November 2016, Orla won a major contract which will immediately bring in additional income of approximately £78,500 per month.

Taxable turnover in the next 30 days alone will be £85,000 (£6,500 + £78,500), which exceeds the threshold, therefore Orla must register for VAT without delay, and her registration will be effective (ie she needs to charge VAT to her customers) immediately.

## Activity 2: Mark – Registration

Mark commenced trading as a carpenter on 1 October 2017. He makes only taxable supplies. The turnover (net of VAT) for each quarter has been shown below. Turnover is spread evenly over the quarter.

| Quarter ended | Turnover £ |
|---|---|
| 31 December 2017 | 17,000 |
| 31 March 2018 | 17,000 |
| 30 June 2018 | 22,800 |
| 30 September 2018 | 24,000 |
| 31 December 2018 | 24,000 |
| 31 March 2019 | 17,000 |

**Required**

(a) When will Mark breach one of the registration tests?

(b) By what date is he required to notify HMRC that he is liable to register for VAT?

(c) When will Mark be registered for VAT?

**Solution:**

## Activity 3: Registration scenarios

You have the following information about the taxable supplies of three businesses.

**Required**

**For each of them, indicate whether they need to register for VAT immediately, or monitor turnover and register later. Tick ONE box on EACH line.**

| | Register now | Monitor and register later |
|---|---|---|
| A A new business with an expected turnover of £8,000 per month for the next 12 months. | | |
| B An existing business with a total turnover of £79,000 for the last 11 months. Sales for the next 30 days are not yet known. | | |
| C An existing business with a total turnover of £7,000 per month for the last 12 months. | | |

**Solution:**

## 2.2 Exemptions from compulsory registration

The registration requirement can be waived under two circumstances:

1    If the business can satisfy HMRC that taxable supplies in the following 12-month period will be less than the deregistration threshold of £81,000.

2    If the business makes only (or mainly) zero-rated supplies.

## Registration decision tree

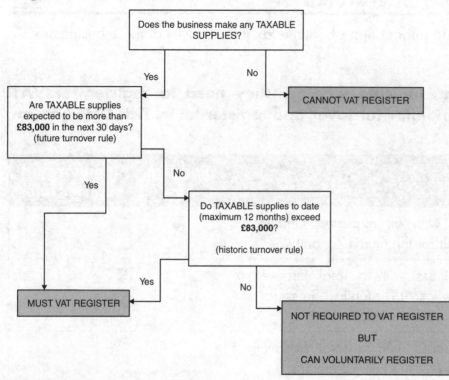

## 2.3 Voluntary registration

A business may apply for VAT registration even though its taxable turnover is below the registration threshold.

Zero-rated traders may choose to register early to produce a net repayment position.

## 2.4 Implications of registration

Some benefits and drawbacks of registration are highlighted below:

| Advantages | Disadvantages |
|---|---|
| • Recover input VAT | • Administration burden |
| • Discipline | • Risk of penalties on errors |
| • Avoid late registration penalty | • Prices go up for non-VAT-registered customers as they cannot reclaim the input VAT on the purchase (need to look at customer status) |

## Activity 4: Voluntary registration

**Required**

**Choose ONE reason why a business making taxable supplies might choose not to register for VAT voluntarily.**

(a)  Preparation of VAT returns would be required
(b)  Customers would benefit by being able to claim back input VAT
(c)  The business would benefit by being able to claim back input VAT

**Solution:**

## 2.5 Deregistration

If the business ceases to make taxable supplies, it **must deregister**. The business must inform HMRC within 30 days of ceasing to make taxable supplies.

A business may **voluntarily** deregister if in the next 12-month period, the VAT exclusive value of taxable supplies will be below £81,000.

## 2.6 Failure to register

If the business fails to register on time, the business will be taxed as if it had registered on time. The business will therefore still owe to HMRC the VAT that it should have been collecting on sales since the date on which registration should have been effective.

The business can calculate this in two ways:

(a)  Treat its sales as VAT inclusive, and pay the VAT out of profits.

(b)  Treat its sales as VAT exclusive and try to get the extra money owed for the VAT from its customers.

## Chapter summary

- There are two types of supply – taxable supplies and exempt supplies.

- In the UK there are three rates of VAT for taxable supplies – the standard rate of 20%, a reduced rate of 5% for certain supplies such as domestic fuel and power, and the zero rate.

- In a VAT-registered business, VAT does not increase the selling prices of either zero-rated supplies or exempt supplies. However, if a business makes exempt supplies, it cannot reclaim the input tax on its purchases and expenses. If the supplies made by the business are zero-rated, then input VAT can be reclaimed.

- The cost of purchases to a VAT-registered business making taxable supplies is generally the VAT-exclusive price. The cost of purchases to a business not registered for VAT, including a business making wholly exempt supplies, is the VAT-inclusive price.

- When a business's taxable turnover reaches the registration limit, then the business must register for VAT; otherwise the business is liable for penalties (see Chapter 7).

- Some businesses may find it advantageous to register for VAT even though the registration limit has not been met – this is known as voluntary registration.

- If a business's taxable turnover falls below the deregistration limit, then the business can apply to HMRC to deregister.

- If a business ceases to make taxable supplies, then it must deregister.

## Keywords

- **Exempt supplies:** supplies on which no VAT is charged

- **Registration:** the process required if a business making taxable supplies must (if it exceeds the registration limits), or wants to, start charging (and recovering) VAT. VAT must be charged on taxable supplies from the date of registration

- **Standard-rated supplies:** goods and services which are taxable at a rate of 20%

- **Taxable turnover:** this is the VAT-exclusive level of standard-rated, reduced rate and zero-rated sales, but excludes exempt sales

- **Zero-rated supplies:** goods and services which are taxable but the rate of tax on them is 0%

## Activity 1: Cost to business

| Business type | Type of supply made | Net cost £ |
|---|---|---|
| Insurance company | Only exempt supplies | 1,200 |
| Accountancy firm | Only standard-rated supplies | 1,000 |
| Bus company | Only zero-rated supplies | 1,000 |

Although the accountancy firm and bus company pay £1,200 for their telephone bills, they are able to reclaim the input VAT of £200, so the net cost is £1,000. The insurance company making exempt supplies is not able to reclaim input tax and so the net cost is £1,200.

## Activity 2: Mark – Registration

(a) As his turnover in the last 12 months does not exceed £83,000 until 31 October 2018 (on a month-by-month basis) he does not become liable until then.

**Working:** 12 months to 30 September = £80,800

12 months to 31 October = £80,800 + (£24,000/3) – (£17,000/3)= £83,133

(b) He must then notify the HM Revenue & Customs within 30 days, ie by 30 November 2018.

(c) He is then registered from 1 December 2018 or an earlier date by mutual agreement.

## Activity 3: Registration scenarios

| | | Register now | Monitor and register later |
|---|---|---|---|
| A | A new business with an expected turnover of £8,000 per month for the next 12 months. | | ✓ |
| B | An existing business with a total turnover of £79,000 for the last 11 months. Sales for the next 30 days are not yet known. | | ✓ |
| C | An existing business with a total turnover of £7,000 per month for the last 12 months. | ✓ | |

A    Monitor and register later, as neither the historic nor the future test have been exceeded at this point

B    Monitor and register later, as taxable supplies have not yet exceeded £83,000 in the last 12 months

C    Register now, as taxable supplies in the previous twelve months exceed £83,000

## Activity 4: Voluntary registration

(a)   (c) is factually correct; but VAT can only be claimed back once registered. (b) is not correct because VAT-registered customers would neither gain nor lose because they could reclaim VAT charged to them, and non-registered customers would be disadvantaged because they would be charged VAT they could not reclaim.

1   **Identify whether the following statements are true or false.**

|  | True ✓ | False ✓ |
|---|---|---|
| If a business supplies zero-rated services, then the business is not able to reclaim the VAT on its purchases and expenses from HMRC. |  |  |
| A business makes zero-rated supplies. The cost to the business of its purchases and expenses is the VAT exclusive amount. |  |  |

2   The following three businesses are trying to decide whether they need to register for VAT immediately, within the next 30 days, or whether they just need to monitor the situation for the time being.

**Tick the correct box for each line.**

|  |  | Register without delay | Register within 30 days | Monitor and register later |
|---|---|---|---|---|
| A | An existing business with total turnover for the previous 11 months of £80,000. Sales for the next month are unknown at present. |  |  |  |
| B | A new business with an expected turnover for the next 30 days of £90,000 |  |  |  |
| C | An existing business with total turnover for the previous 12 months of £7,250 per month |  |  |  |

3   You have been contacted by a potential new client, Mrs Quirke. She has recently started trading as an interior designer.

**By selecting from the options listed, complete the following letter to her, explaining when her business must register for VAT.**

AN Accountant
Number Street
London
SW11 8AB

Mrs Quirke
Alphabet Street
London
W12 6WM

Dear Mrs Quirke

VAT REGISTRATION

Further to our recent telephone conversation, set out below are the circumstances when you must register your business for VAT.

If the taxable turnover of your business at the end of a month, looking back no more than (1) [_____▼] months, has exceeded the registration limit of (2) [£ _____▼] then the business must apply to register for VAT within 30 days.

Alternatively, if at any time the taxable turnover (before any VAT is added) is expected to exceed the registration limit within the next (3) [_____▼] alone, then the business must apply to be registered for VAT without delay. This would be the situation if, for example, you obtained a large additional contract for, say, £85,000.

If you wish to discuss this in any more detail, please do not hesitate to contact me.

Yours sincerely

AN Accountant

**Picklists:**

(1)   six / 12 / 24

(2)   £81,000 / £83,000

(3)   week / 30 days / 12 months

4   Amy started trading on 1 August 2016. Her monthly sales (excluding VAT) are:

|  | £ |
|---|---|
| Standard-rated supplies | 7,850 |
| Zero-rated supplies | 1,470 |
| Exempt supplies | 700 |
|  | 10,020 |

**By what date will Amy exceed the threshold for VAT?**

|  |
|---|
|  |

**By what date must Amy register for VAT?**

|  |
|---|
|  |

5   Richard made taxable supplies of £72,500 in his first 11 months of trading. His taxable supplies in month 12 are £11,000.

**Which of the following explains why Richard must register for VAT? Tick ONE box.**

|  | ✓ |
|---|---|
| At the beginning of month 12, Richard expects his taxable supplies to exceed £83,000 in the next 30 days. |  |
| At the end of month 12, Richard's taxable supplies in the previous 12 months will have exceeded £83,000. |  |

6   **Decide why a business making taxable supplies might choose to register for VAT voluntarily. Tick ONE box.**

|  | ✓ |
|---|---|
| Preparation of VAT returns would be optional |  |
| Customers would benefit by being able to claim back input VAT |  |
| Business would benefit by being able to claim back input VAT |  |

# Inputs and outputs

## Learning outcomes

Having studied this chapter you will be able to:

| 2.2 | Calculate the VAT arising when given the net or gross amount of a supply |
|-----|--------------------------------------------------------------------------|
| | • Account for VAT on: expenditure on employee and business contact entertaining, purchases and sales of cars and vans |
| | • Understand the VAT rules on fuel scale charges, how to apply them and their effect on VAT payable or reclaimable |
| | • Understand how partial exemption works, the *de minimis* limit and how this effects the recovery of input tax |
| | • Calculate VAT for imports and acquisitions, exports and despatches |
| | • Identify the place of supply rules for both goods and services within and outside the EU |
| | • Understand how imports, acquisitions, despatches and exports are treated on a VAT return |

## Assessment context

Calculating and interpreting VAT is core to this unit. You will need to know how VAT is affected by different types of transactions. There is lots of information available in the reference material which will be available during the exam.

Task 4 (AQ13) will examine detailed VAT rules.

Task 5 will examine detailed VAT calculations.

## Qualification context

You should be aware of the fact that the calculation of VAT changes depending on the type of transaction.

## Business context

Every registered business needs to account for VAT accurately using the rules set out by the VAT legislation. These rules are some of the basics that you will need to be aware of in business.

# Chapter overview

**Calculation of VAT**
- Inclusive of VAT
- Exclusive of VAT

**Irrecoverable input VAT**
- Business entertaining
- Cars
- Private use items

**Partially exempt traders**
- Make taxable and exempt supplies
- *De minimis* test needed to identify how much input VAT can be recovered

**Overseas transactions**
- Imports
- Exports
- Despatches
- Acquisitions

# 1 Calculating VAT

VAT charged on taxable supplies is based on the VAT exclusive value.

Prices given to you by the examiner can be either inclusive (gross) or exclusive (net) of VAT. (You will always be told which is the case.)

**Formula to learn**

If an invoice shows that a standard-rated supply (VAT at 20%) has a **VAT exclusive** amount of £100.00 then the VAT is calculated as:

£100.00 × 20% = £20.00

If an invoice shows that a standard-rated supply has a **VAT inclusive** amount of £120.00, the amount of VAT can be calculated in one of two ways:

Either:

£120.00 × 20/120 = £20.00 or,

£120.00 × 1/6 = £20.00

| Type of supply | Apply to 'net' value (VAT exclusive) | Apply to 'gross' value (VAT inclusive) |
|---|---|---|
| Standard-rated supply | 20% | 1/6 (20/120) |
| Reduced-rated supply (AQ16 only) | 5% | 5/105 |

**Illustration 1: Calculation of VAT**

An invoice shows a total VAT inclusive (gross) amount of £48.00. The amount of VAT at 20% included in this amount can be calculated as follows:

£48.00 × 20/120 = £8.00

or

£48.00 × 1/6 = £8.00

You can check this working by applying the 20% to the VAT exclusive (net) amount:

£48.00 less £8.00 (VAT worked out above) = £40.00 (net amount)

£40.00 × 20% = £8.00

## Activity 1: Calculation of VAT – Inclusive price

VAT inclusive price = £642.00 (standard rate @ 20%).

**Required**

**Calculate the VAT.**

**Solution:**

## 1.1 Rounding of VAT

Any VAT calculation should normally be rounded down to the nearest penny. (This concession is not available to retailers.)

## Activity 2: Calculation of VAT – Rounding

An item has a net value of £54.89.

**Required**

**How much VAT (@ 20%) should be charged on this item?**

**Solution:**

## 1.2 VAT payable to HMRC

Each VAT period (see later) a taxable person will need to calculate how much VAT is owed to/repayable from HMRC.

| This is calculated as: | £ |
|---|---|
| Output VAT | X |
| Less: | |
| Input VAT | (X) |
| VAT Payable/(Repayable) | X/(X) |

## Activity 3: Calculation of VAT – VAT payable

A business buys goods for £1,000 excluding 20% VAT. It then sells those goods for £1,800 inclusive of 20% VAT.

**Required**

**What is the total VAT paid to or reclaimed from the HMRC?**

**Choose one:**

A    £200 paid

B    £300 reclaimed

C    £100 paid

D    £100 reclaimed

**Solution:**

Usually (when input tax is recoverable), the cost to a VAT-registered business of buying goods and services is the **VAT-exclusive (net) amount**. For example:

|  | £ |
|---|---|
| Amount paid to supplier (VAT-inclusive) | 1,200 |
| Input VAT reclaimed from HMRC | (200) |
| Net cost to the business (VAT-exclusive) | 1,000 |

However, in certain circumstances, a business may not be able to recover all the input tax it has incurred on its purchases. Where VAT is irrecoverable, the cost to the business is the **VAT-inclusive amount.**

## 2 Irrecoverable input VAT

If a taxable person (one who is making taxable supplies – standard, reduced or zero-rated) is registered for VAT, then they will be able to recover their input VAT. There are, however, some circumstances where input VAT cannot be recovered.

## 2.1 Business entertaining

The input VAT incurred on business entertaining is not recoverable from HMRC. Business entertaining however, does not include the following:

(a) Staff entertaining
(b) Entertaining of non-UK customers.

The recovery of input VAT, where there is a mixed group of staff and non-staff being entertained, would be apportioned appropriately.

## 2.2 Cars and vans

Unless a car is used exclusively for business purposes, then none of the input VAT, including the VAT on car accessories purchased at the same time, will be recoverable. (There will be no output VAT charged on disposal either as this will be an exempt supply.)

There are some exceptions to this, for example, cars used:

- Exclusively for business purposes (eg pool cars)
- Within a taxi business
- For driving instruction
- Within a self-drive hire business.

In the assessment, you will need to assume that the car has some private use unless told otherwise.

When purchasing a van, as long as the van is used at least partly to make taxable supplies, then the input VAT will be recoverable. For this reason, when the van is sold, then output VAT would need to be charged on disposal.

| Capital item | Input tax recoverable on purchase? | Output tax chargeable on sale of item? |
|---|---|---|
| New car for employee's use | NO | NO – Exempt |
| Car used in taxi business | YES | YES |
| Van | YES | YES |

## Activity 4: Reclaiming input tax

Identify whether input tax can be reclaimed by a VAT-registered business in each of the following circumstances.

| Circumstance | Yes, can reclaim ✓ | No, cannot reclaim ✓ |
|---|---|---|
| Input tax incurred entertaining prospective new UK client | | |
| Input tax incurred on a new car for the top salesperson | | |
| Input tax incurred on a car for use in a driving instruction business | | |

## 2.3 Private use

If an item purchased is being used for business and private purposes, then the portion of input VAT relating to the private use would not be recoverable.

## 2.4 Fuel for private use

Input tax on all road fuel purchased by the business and used for business purposes can be reclaimed.

However, when a taxable person purchases fuel and it is used for private motoring by an employee or the sole trader/partner, then this has an impact on the recoverability of the input VAT. The taxable person has a number of options:

(a) Ensure that the individual keeps sufficient mileage records so that the input VAT on just the business miles can be recovered

(b) Reclaim all the input VAT suffered on fuel but then account for some **output VAT** using a set **fuel scale charge** per quarter. This scale charge is based on the $CO_2$ emission of the vehicle, and will be given to you in the exam if needed.

(c) Agree not to reclaim any input VAT on fuel purchased for any (including commercial) vehicles.

## Activity 5: Reclaiming input tax on private fuel

**Decide whether each of the following statements is true or false.**

| | True ✓ | False ✓ |
|---|---|---|
| A VAT-registered business can reclaim all the input VAT on road fuel if it keeps detailed records of business and private mileage, and makes no other adjustment. | | |
| A VAT-registered business can reclaim all the input VAT on road fuel if it pays the appropriate fuel scale charge for private mileage. | | |

## 2.5 Partially exempt traders

How much input VAT a taxable person can reclaim is determined by the type of supplies they make, as discussed earlier in the syllabus.

A taxable trader making only taxable supplies (standard, reduced or zero-rated), can reclaim all their input VAT, subject to the exceptions noted above.

An exempt trader, making only exempt supplies, cannot reclaim any of their input VAT.

There are, however, some traders who make both taxable and exempt supplies. These are called **partially exempt traders**.

Partially exempt traders:

(a) Only charge output VAT on their taxable supplies

(b) Can reclaim the input VAT on all purchases directly related to taxable supplies

(c) Can reclaim a proportion of input VAT which is not directly attributable to taxable or exempt supplies. This is based on the following calculation:

$$\text{Input VAT not directly attributable to taxable or exempt supplies} \times \left[ \frac{\text{Value of taxable supplies made}}{\text{Total supplies made (taxable and exempt)}} \right]*$$

**\* round up to nearest percent**

The rest of the input VAT is only recoverable if it is below the **de minimis limit**; the amount is below £625 per month on average, **and** it is ≤ 50% of the total input tax for the period.

Note that your assessment will not test the detailed calculations. However, the following table should aid your understanding.

| Input tax | Recoverable | Not recoverable |
|---|---|---|
| Directly attributed to taxable supplies | ✓ | |
| Directly attributed to exempt supplies | | ✗ |
| Indirectly attributed (split-using calculation) | ✓ | ✗ |
| | ✓ | ✗ ← UNLESS below *de minimis* limits |

## Activity 6: Partially exempt trader – Calculation

For the quarter ended 30 June 20X9, Jim has allocated his input tax suffered between taxable and exempt supplies, but a balance remains unallocated.

| Exempt | Taxable | Unallocated | Total input tax |
|---|---|---|---|
| £ | £ | £ | £ |
| 700 | 20,000 | 3,000 | 23,700 |

His total turnover for the quarter was £135,429 of which taxable supplies amounted to £114,573.

**Required**

**How much of the £23,700 input tax suffered is recoverable by Jim?**

**Solution:**

*Attributable to taxable supplies*

| | £ |
|---|---|
| Directly allocated | |
| Indirectly allocated: | |
| | |
| | |
| *Attributable to exempt supplies* | |
| | |
| Directly allocated | |
| Indirectly allocated: | |
| | |
| | |

35

## Activity 7: Partially exempt trader – Multiple choice

A business supplies goods that are a mixture of standard-rated, exempt and zero-rated.

**Required**

**Which of the following statements is true? Choose ONE answer.**

A    All of the input VAT can be reclaimed

B    None of the input VAT can be reclaimed

C    All of the input VAT can be reclaimed, providing certain *(de minimis)* conditions are met

D    Some of the input VAT can be reclaimed, in proportion to the different types of supply

**Solution:**

# 3 Overseas Transactions

Please note these rules are, as yet, unchanged since the EU referendum.

## 3.1 Determining the place of supply

UK VAT is charged on supplies within the UK. It is therefore important to understand whether or not a supply is 'in the UK' – this is determined by the "place of supply" rules.

**Goods** are deemed to be supplied where they 'originate', or start their journey. If they are located in the UK before being shipped to a customer, the place of supply is the UK.

**Services** are a little more complex; if the supply is to a registered business customer (for example, the performance of a company audit by its external auditors), they are deemed to be supplied where the customer is located. Other supplies of services (to non-registered businesses or consumers) are deemed to be supplied in the seller's country.

## 3.2 Within EU

Supplies of goods to EU countries are referred to as **despatches** and are zero-rated if the trader obtains the customer's VAT number and can prove the goods left the UK. Otherwise, tax at the UK rate (ie 20%).

When goods are purchased from elsewhere in the EU, this is referred to as an **acquisition**; no VAT is charged by the supplier. The UK purchaser has to charge themselves output VAT on the VAT return. This is then offset by an equal amount of input VAT. For a fully taxable trader, the transaction is therefore VAT neutral.

## Outside EU

If goods are supplied to countries outside of the EU, they are referred to as **exports** and are always zero-rated, provided the trader obtains evidence of their export within three months.

Goods which are purchased from countries outside of the EU are known as **imports**. No VAT is charged by the supplier. When the goods enter the UK, the purchaser needs to pay the applicable rate of UK VAT.

## Activity 8: Despatches

A UK VAT-registered trader sells goods to both VAT-registered and non VAT-registered traders elsewhere in the EU. If these goods had been sold in the UK, they would have been standard-rated.

**Required**

**Which of the following is the correct treatment assuming all other conditions are fulfilled? Tick ONE box.**

| To VAT-registered traders | To non-VAT-registered traders | ✓ |
|---|---|---|
| Zero-rated | Zero-rated | |
| Standard-rated | Zero-rated | |
| Zero-rated | Standard-rated | |
| Standard-rated | Standard-rated | |

# Chapter summary

- VAT is charged on standard-rated supplies at 20%. The VAT amount in a VAT-inclusive price is found by multiplying by 1/6.

- The VAT on business entertainment expenses of UK customers and (usually) on the purchase of cars for use within a business is non-reclaimable.

- If input VAT is reclaimed on fuel used for private journeys, an amount of output VAT (the fuel scale charge) also has to be charged.

- If a VAT-registered business makes both taxable and exempt supplies, it is partially exempt. The recovery of input tax will be restricted, subject to the *de minimis* limits.

- Goods imported from outside the EU are charged at the same rate as goods in the UK. The tax is paid by the trader at the port or airport.

- The VAT on acquisitions of goods from other EU countries is treated as both output tax and input tax.

- Exports of goods to another country outside the EU are treated as zero-rated supplies.

- Despatches of goods to other EU countries are usually zero-rated if the customer is VAT-registered, and has provided their VAT-registration number. Otherwise, they are treated as if they were normal UK sales.

## Keywords

- **Acquisitions:** goods purchased from another European Union country

- **Despatches:** goods sold to another European Union country

- **Exports:** goods sold to a country outside the European Union

- **Fuel scale charge:** an output VAT charge to offset against the input VAT reclaimed on fuel purchased for private use

- **Imports:** goods purchased from a country outside the European Union

- **Partial exemption:** when a business makes a mixture of taxable and exempt supplies then input VAT attributable to exempt supplies may only be reclaimed subject to satisfying *de minimis* tests

BPP
LEARNING MEDIA

## Activity answers

### Activity 1: Calculation of VAT – Inclusive price

VAT $= 642.00 \times \dfrac{1}{6}$

$\qquad = £107.00$

### Activity 2: Calculation of VAT – Rounding

VAT $= £54.89 \times 20\%$

$\qquad = £10.978$

$\qquad = £10.97$ (rounded down to the nearest penny)

### Activity 3: Calculation of VAT – VAT payable

C      A is the amount deductible, B is the amount payable.

**Working**

|  | £ |
|---|---|
| Output tax £1,800 x 1/6 | 300 |
| Input tax £1,000 x 20% | (200) |
| VAT payable | 100 |

### Activity 4: Reclaiming input tax

| Circumstance | Yes, can reclaim ✓ | No, cannot reclaim ✓ |
|---|---|---|
| Input tax incurred entertaining prospective new UK client | | ✓ |
| Input tax incurred on a new car for the top salesperson | | ✓ |
| Input tax incurred on a car for use in a driving instruction business | ✓ | |

## Activity 5: Reclaiming input tax on private fuel

|  | True ✓ | False ✓ |
|---|---|---|
| A VAT-registered business can reclaim all the input VAT on road fuel if it keeps detailed records of business and private mileage, and makes no other adjustment. |  | ✓ |
| A VAT-registered business can reclaim all the input VAT on road fuel if it pays the appropriate fuel scale charge for private mileage. | ✓ |  |

## Activity 6: Partially exempt trader – Calculation

*Attributable to taxable supplies*

|  | £ |
|---|---|
| Directly allocated | 20,000 |
| Indirectly allocated: |  |
| $3,000 \times \dfrac{114,573}{135,429}$ (85%) | 2,550 |
|  | Recoverable 22,550 |
| *Attributable to exempt supplies* |  |
|  | £ |
| Directly allocated | 700 |
| Indirectly allocated: |  |
| (3,000 – 2,550) | 450 |
|  | 1,150 |

### Workings

Monthly average    = 1,150 ÷ 3
                     = £383

This is < £625 per month.

Total input tax = £23,700. Relating to taxable supplies = £22,550 (above).

This is > 50%

Therefore all of the £1,150 exempt input tax is recoverable as well as the £22,550 attributed to taxable supplies.

## Activity 7: Partially exempt trader – Multiple choice

C    All of the input VAT can be reclaimed, providing certain *(de minimis)* conditions are met.

## Activity 8: Despatches

| To VAT-registered traders | To non-VAT-registered traders | ✓ |
| --- | --- | --- |
| Zero-rated | Zero-rated | |
| Standard-rated | Zero-rated | |
| Zero-rated | Standard-rated | ✓ |
| Standard-rated | Standard-rated | |

## Test your learning

1 Business C sells goods to Business D for £384.00 plus the standard rate of VAT. Both businesses are VAT-registered.

(a) **What amount of VAT will be charged on this transaction?**

| The VAT is | £ |
|---|---|

(b) **Which business will treat the VAT as output tax and which will treat it as input tax?**

| | Output tax ✓ | Input tax ✓ |
|---|---|---|
| Business C | | |
| Business D | | |

2 **Identify which TWO of the following types of expenditure have irrecoverable input tax.**

| | ✓ |
|---|---|
| Staff party | |
| Car for sales manager | |
| Photocopier | |
| Entertaining UK clients | |

3 You have received four invoices from suppliers which show only the total VAT-inclusive price and the fact that all of the goods are standard-rated.

**For each invoice total, determine the amount of VAT that is included.**

**Complete the following table.**

| VAT-inclusive £ | VAT at 20 % £ |
|---|---|
| 42.88 | |
| 96.57 | |
| 28.20 | |
| 81.07 | |

4   A UK VAT-registered business is exporting goods which are standard-rated in the UK to an American business.

**Which ONE of the following statements is correct? Tick the relevant box.**

|  | ✓ |
|---|---|
| The goods will be treated as standard-rated in the UK if the American business is VAT-registered. |  |
| The goods will be treated as standard-rated in the UK, provided documentary evidence of the export is obtained within three months. |  |
| The goods will be treated as zero-rated in the UK if the American business is VAT-registered. |  |
| The goods will be treated as zero-rated in the UK, provided documentary evidence of the export is obtained within three months. |  |

5   **Complete the following table.**

| Net £ | VAT rate % | VAT £ | Gross £ |
|---|---|---|---|
|  | 20 |  | 52.20 |
| 18.00 | 20 |  |  |

6   **Decide whether each of the following statements is true or false.**

|  | True ✓ | False ✓ |
|---|---|---|
| A VAT-registered business can reclaim all the input VAT attributed to zero-rated supplies. |  |  |
| A VAT-registered business can reclaim all the input VAT attributed to standard-rated supplies. |  |  |
| A VAT-registered business can reclaim all the input VAT attributed to exempt supplies. |  |  |
| A VAT-registered business can reclaim all the input VAT attributed to both taxable and exempt supplies, providing certain *de minimis* tests are satisfied. |  |  |

7   Joe, a VAT-registered trader, acquires goods from a VAT-registered supplier in another EU country.

**Tick the box that describes how Joe should deal with this acquisition for VAT.**

| | ✓ |
|---|---|
| No VAT is charged by the EU supplier; therefore this can be ignored by Joe on his VAT return. | |
| Joe must pay output VAT to HMRC at the port/airport and can reclaim input VAT on the next return. | |
| Joe must charge himself 'output VAT' and 'reclaim input' VAT on the same return. | |

# Accounting for VAT

## Learning outcomes

Having studied this chapter you will be able to:

| 1.2 | Explain the tax authority's rules about: what constitute VAT records; how long VAT records should be retained; how VAT records should be retained. |
|-----|---------------------------------------------------------------------------------------------------------------------------------------------------|
| 1.4 | Identify the correct contents and form of a VAT invoice, including:<br><br>• The simplified VAT invoice rule<br><br>• Determine the tax point of an invoice, both basic and actual, when the invoice is raised after the supply and also when there are: advance payments; deposits; continuous supplies; and goods on sale or return<br><br>• The significance of the correct tax point for eligibility for special VAT schemes, applying the correct rate of VAT and determining the correct VAT for reporting<br><br>• The time limits for issuing VAT invoices, including understanding the 14-day and 30-day rules |
| 2.1 | Extract relevant data from the accounting records including:<br><br>• How to identify relevant accounting records that cover the required period of each VAT return<br><br>• How to identify and extract relevant income, expenditure and VAT figures from the following ledgers and accounts: sales and sales returns, purchases and purchases returns; cash and petty cash accounts; and the VAT account<br><br>• Understand the impact of credit notes and debit notes |
| 2.2 | Identify how to apply bad debt relief, when this is available and what time limits apply |

## Assessment context

You will need to be able to explain how different VAT transactions are treated when they are accounted for and how the VAT payable to HMRC will be affected by each transaction.

Task 1 may include a question about VAT records.

Task 2 will involve questions about VAT invoices. This task may also involve a scenario in which you need to determine the tax point of a transaction.

Task 3 could look into bad debt relief which is discussed at the end of this chapter.

# Qualification context

This section of the notes will use your knowledge of a business's accounts. It is this information which will be used to produce the VAT return.

# Business context

The accounting system within the business will need to store information which can be extracted in order to produce the VAT return. It is therefore important to know how the VAT transactions will be accounted for.

# Chapter overview

**Accounting for VAT**

**VAT records**

- Accounting records
- VAT invoices
- Simplified VAT invoices

**Timing**

- Tax point
- Date used to account for VAT
- Bad debt relief

# 1 Keeping records

## 1.1 VAT records

It is essential that businesses keep a record of all their transactions. Amongst other reasons, this is so that they are able to prove to HMRC that the level of input VAT which has been reclaimed is accurate. HMRC may also want to verify that the level of output VAT which has been paid has also been calculated correctly.

Generally the information that a VAT-registered business **must** keep includes:

- Business and accounting records
- Invoices issued and received in respect of transactions within the UK, acquisitions, despatches, imports and exports
- Credit/debit notes issued and received
- VAT account summarising output VAT and input VAT.

The records which are kept should relate to both the **exempt and taxable** goods and services which the business has received and supplied.

The accounting records that most businesses keep in order to verify their sales include:

- **Sales day book** – this is a record of all of the invoices sent out to credit customers showing the net amount of the sale, the VAT and the invoice total.
- **Sales returns day book** – this is a record of all of the credit notes sent out to credit customers, or debit notes received from credit customers, for returns and alterations to invoice amounts.
- **Cash receipts book** – this records receipts from credit customers as well as other receipts for cash sales.
- Orders and delivery notes, bank statements and paying-in slips.

The accounting records that most businesses keep in order to verify their purchases include:

- **Purchases day book** – this is a record of all of the invoices received from credit suppliers.
- **Purchases returns day book** – this is a record of all of the credit notes received by the business and any debit notes issued.
- **Cash and petty cash payments book** – this is a record of all of the cash payments made by the business.

All records need to be kept for a minimum of **six years** and HMRC is entitled to inspect these records at any time. The supporting information for the VAT returns must be easy to find.

These lists of required records are in the reference material provided for you in the exam.

## 1.2 VAT invoice

VAT-registered businesses must raise a **VAT invoice** (paper or electronic) when they make a taxable supply to another VAT-registered business.

If the customer is not VAT-registered, then a VAT invoice is not mandatory, unless requested by the customer.

The invoice needs to be raised within 30 days of the supply. If an invoice is not raised, then the supplier has failed to keep proper records, and may have filed an incorrect VAT return, both of which carry potential penalties.

A taxable person can only reclaim input VAT if they have a valid VAT invoice for the purchase.

An example invoice is shown below:

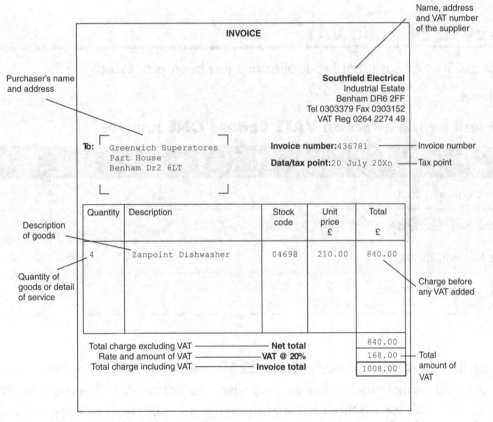

A VAT invoice must show all the information marked above. This list is included in the AAT reference material provided to you in the assessment.

## Activity 1: Valid VAT invoice

**Using your AAT reference material, which three of the following items must be included on a valid VAT invoice?**

|  | ✓ |
|---|---|
| Customer VAT registration number | |
| Supplier VAT registration number | |
| Total VAT-exclusive amount for each type of item sold | |
| Total VAT amount for each type of item sold | |
| Total VAT-inclusive amount for each type of item sold | |

## Activity 2: Effect on VAT

A purchase invoice for taxable supplies has just been processed.

**Required**

**What will be the effect on VAT? Choose ONE answer.**

|  | ✓ |
|---|---|
| Input tax will increase | |
| Input tax will decrease | |
| Output tax will increase | |
| Output tax will decrease | |

For **supplies invoiced at less than £250**, including VAT, a business may issue a less detailed **simplified invoice**. Suppliers do not need to keep copies of these simplified VAT invoices, although the customer would still need to keep the invoice if they wanted to reclaim the input VAT.

The reduced detail required on a simplified invoice is listed in the AAT reference material.

If the expenditure total is £25 or less including VAT, then no invoice is required to reclaim VAT for:

- Telephone calls or car park fees
- Purchases made through coin operated machines.

## 1.3 Pro forma invoice

A **pro forma invoice** is often used in order to offer goods to a potential customer at a certain price and to invite the customer to send a payment, in return for which the goods will be despatched.

Businesses are not allowed to use this to reclaim input VAT and as such, any proforma invoice should be clearly marked 'THIS IS NOT A VAT INVOICE'.

If the customer does decide to buy the goods or sends payment, then a proper VAT invoice must be issued within 30 days of the supply or payment (if earlier).

## Activity 3: Reclaiming input VAT

**Decide whether the following statements are true or false. Tick the relevant boxes below.**

|  | True ✓ | False ✓ |
|---|---|---|
| A 'simplified' invoice can be used to reclaim input VAT |  |  |
| A 'pro forma' invoice can be used to reclaim input VAT |  |  |

# 2 VAT and discounts

Many businesses offer discounts to their customers.

There are two types:

(1) **Trade discounts**

    (a) Given at the time of the sale/purchase, they reduce the selling price as an inducement to purchase

    (b) Usually for regular customers or **bulk buyers**.

(2) **Settlement discounts** – these are not currently on the AQ13 syllabus.

    **For AQ16 students only:**

    If a supplier offers a settlement discount (a reduced price as an inducement to pay earlier than the normal credit terms), the VAT charged must be based on the actual consideration received. There are three ways of achieving this:

    (a) Issue the invoice based on the discounted amount, and a further invoice for the difference once the discount period has expired

    (b) Issue an invoice for the full amount, followed by a credit note if the discount is taken up

    (c) Issue one invoice, with both possible prices and VAT amounts specified, with clear instructions to the customer regarding recoverability of their input VAT.

## Activity 4: Settlement discounts

A business sells goods for £1000 plus VAT, but allows a settlement discount of 5% for payment within 10 days. The customer pays after 8 days. The trader had decided to invoice for the full amount.

**Required**

**What is the correct action for the trader?**

|  | ✓ |
| --- | --- |
| Issue a further invoice for £50 plus VAT |  |
| Issue a credit note for £50 plus VAT |  |
| Take no action |  |
| Issue a credit note for £50 including VAT |  |

**Assessment focus points**

VAT is calculated on the amount after trade discounts.

If you are sitting the AQ16 assessment, remember to look for the actual amount the customer pays if you are asked for the amount of VAT on a transaction.

# 3 Credit notes and debit notes

Once issued, a VAT invoice cannot be amended. Amending an invoice can be viewed as an act of fraud.

Instead, additional documentation needs to be created if anything about the supply needs to be amended.

If the goods have been returned by the customer or the supplier has charged too much, then the supplier may raise a credit note to offset all or part of the original invoice (including the VAT element).

The credit note will decrease output VAT and will therefore reduce the amount payable to HMRC.

Alternatively, the customer could raise a debit note which would have the same impact.

If too little was charged on the original invoice, a separate invoice should be raised for the difference.

## Activity 5: Credit note

A business issues a credit note to a customer.

**Required**

**Which of the following statements is correct for the business?**

|  | ✓ |
|---|---|
| Input tax will increase |  |
| Input tax will decrease |  |
| Output tax will increase |  |
| Output tax will decrease |  |

# 4 Tax point

It is possible that an order could be received, despatched, invoiced and payment made all in different quarters.

The **tax point** rules enable us to determine in which quarter to record the supply or purchase.

(1)   The tax point is the earliest of the following events:

- Despatch/goods made available/service completed (the **basic tax point**)

- Invoice issued

- Payment received

(The order date is irrelevant.)

(2)   If the basic tax point is the earliest date, then check if the invoice was issued within 14 days of that date. If it was, then the invoice date overrides the basic tax point and becomes the **actual tax point**.

Businesses may contact their VAT Business Centre and obtain their agreement in order to have the 14 day rule extended.

The following decision tree should help you to identify the relevant tax point of a transaction.

First, though, you need to identify the following three dates:

- BASIC TAX POINT (date of physical supply)
- Invoice date
- Payment date.

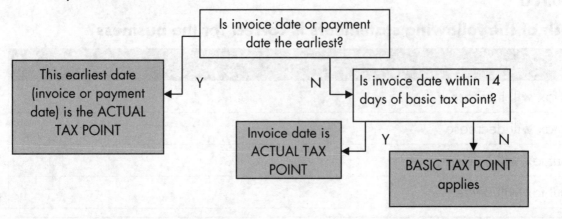

## Activity 6: Alex – Tax point

Alex raises a pro forma invoice and receives a payment in advance of making a supply. The pro forma invoice was dated 18 May X2. The payment was received on 25 May X2. The goods were supplied on 29 May X2 and the VAT invoice was raised on 1 June X2.

**Required**

**What is the tax point? Choose ONE answer.**

A    18 May X2

B    25 May X2

C    29 May X2

D    1 June X2

**Solution:**

If a deposit is paid separately from the balance, then two tax points must be identified.

## Illustration 1: Tax point for deposits

On 1 August, a customer sent in a 15% deposit with an order. The goods were sent out to the customer on 6 August, and an invoice issued on 25 August. The customer paid the remaining 85% on 30 September.

The tax point for the deposit is determined by looking at:

- The basic tax point (delivery date)     6 August
- The invoice date                        25 August
- The deposit payment date                1 August

The actual tax point is created at 1 August, as this is the earliest date.

The tax point for payment of the balance is determined by looking at:

- The basic tax point (delivery date)     6 August
- The invoice date                        25 August
- The date of payment of the balance      30 September

The basic tax point is the earliest date. As the invoice date is more than 14 days after the basic tax point, the invoice date does not override.

Tax point for the balance is 6 August (basic tax point)

## Activity 7: Bang Ltd – Tax point

On 31 May 20X1, Bang Ltd ordered a new printing machine and on 16 June 20X1, paid a deposit of £6,000. The machine was despatched to Bang Ltd on 30 June 20X1. On 18 July 20X1, an invoice was issued to Bang Ltd, showing the full amount and the balance due of £54,000. This was paid on 23 July 20X1.

**Required**

**(a) What is the tax point for the £6,000 deposit? Choose ONE answer.**

    A   16 June 20X1
    B   18 July 20X1
    C   30 June 20X1
    D   23 July 20X1

**(b) What is the tax point for the balance of £54,000? Choose ONE answer.**

    A   16 June 20X1
    B   18 July 20X1
    C   30 June 20X1
    D   23 July 20X1

**Solution:**

# 5 VAT and bad debts

As a result of the tax point rules, output VAT is often paid over to HMRC before payment has been received from customers. If a debt subsequently goes bad, traders can reclaim VAT already accounted for.

All of the following conditions must be met for VAT **bad debt relief** to be available:

(a)   The debt is over six months old (measured from when payment is due), and less than four and a half years old

(b)   The debt has been written off in the trader's books

(c)   The VAT must have been paid to HMRC.

The VAT being reclaimed on the bad debt is recorded as input VAT, rather than a reduction in output VAT.

These conditions are listed in the AAT reference material.

## Activity 8: Bad debt relief

**What effect will claiming VAT bad debt relief have on the amount of VAT due to HMRC? Choose ONE answer.**

|  | ✓ |
|---|---|
| The amount payable will increase |  |
| The amount payable will decrease |  |

## Chapter summary

- All VAT-registered persons must keep full records of the details of all trade, both within the EU and outside the EU; and details of all standard-rated, reduced-rate, zero-rated and exempt goods and services, both purchased and sold.

- These records should normally be kept for six years and must be made available to an HMRC officer if required.

- Copies of sales invoices must be kept and the main accounting records for sales will be the sales day book, sales returns day book and the cash book.

- All invoices for purchases and expenses must be kept; otherwise the input VAT cannot be reclaimed – the main accounting records for purchases and expenses are the purchases day book, the purchases returns day book and the cash book.

- A VAT-registered business making a supply to another VAT-registered business must issue a valid VAT invoice within 30 days of making the supply.

- If goods are supplied for no more than £250, including VAT, a simplified (less detailed) VAT invoice can be issued, which shows only the VAT inclusive amount and the rate of VAT – however, if the customer asks for a full VAT invoice, this must be supplied.

- If a pro forma invoice is sent out to a potential customer, this must be clearly marked 'This is not a VAT invoice' as the customer cannot use it to reclaim any input VAT.

- The basic tax point is the date of physical supply. This basic tax point can be over-ridden by the actual tax point. The actual tax point can be created if an invoice is issued or a payment received before the basic tax point, or by sending out an invoice within 14 days of the basic tax point.

- If a business writes-off a bad debt that is more than six months overdue and the output VAT on the supply has already been paid to HMRC, this VAT can be reclaimed from HMRC as input tax.

## Keywords

- **Actual tax point:** a further date that can override the basic tax point if certain conditions are met

- **Bad debt relief:** a reclaim of output VAT when a written-off debt is more than six months overdue

- **Basic tax point:** the date on which goods are delivered or services provided

- **Cash books:** a record of all payments and receipts of the business

- **Pro forma invoice:** often used to offer goods to potential customers. It is not a valid VAT invoice.

- **Purchases day book:** a record of all invoices received from credit suppliers

- **Purchases returns day book:** a record of all credit notes received from credit suppliers

- **Sales day book:** a record of all invoices sent to credit customers

- **Sales returns day book:** a record of all credit notes sent to credit customers

- **Simplified (less detailed) invoice:** an invoice that can be issued if the VAT-inclusive value of goods supplied is no more than £250

- **Tax point:** the date which determines when the VAT must be accounted for to HMRC

- **VAT invoice:** a document that allows input VAT to be claimed or output VAT to be charged

BPP
LEARNING MEDIA

## Activity answers

### Activity 1: Valid VAT invoice

| | ✓ |
|---|---|
| Customer VAT registration number | |
| Supplier VAT registration number | ✓ |
| Total VAT-exclusive amount for each type of item sold | ✓ |
| Total VAT amount for each type of item sold | ✓ |
| Total VAT-inclusive amount for each type of item sold | |

### Activity 2: Effect on VAT

| | ✓ |
|---|---|
| Input tax will increase | ✓ |
| Input tax will decrease | |
| Output tax will increase | |
| Output tax will decrease | |

### Activity 3: Reclaiming input VAT

| | True ✓ | False ✓ |
|---|---|---|
| A 'simplified' invoice can be used to reclaim input VAT | ✓ | |
| A 'proforma' invoice can be used to reclaim input VAT | | ✓ |

### Activity 4: Settlement discounts

| | ✓ |
|---|---|
| Issue a further invoice for £50 plus VAT | |
| Issue a credit note for £50 plus VAT | ✓ |
| Take no action | |
| Issue a credit note for £50 including VAT | |

## Activity 5: Credit note

| | ✓ |
|---|---|
| Input tax will increase | |
| Input tax will decrease | |
| Output tax will increase | |
| Output tax will decrease | ✓ |

## Activity 6: Alex – Tax point

B    25 May X2

Ignore the pro forma invoice (as this is not a VAT invoice).

The earliest date is then the payment date, which is therefore the actual tax point.

(Only the despatch date (basic tax point) is ever over ridden by the invoice date.)

## Activity 7: Bang ltd – Tax point

(a)    A    16 June 20X1

    The deposit payment is the earliest date (ignoring the order date). This is never over ridden by the invoice date.

(b)    C    30 June 20X1

    The despatch date is the earliest date relating to the balancing payment. Double check if the invoice is issued within 14 days. In this case, it is not; therefore the despatch date remains as the tax point.

## Activity 8: Bad debt reliefs

| | ✓ |
|---|---|
| The amount payable will increase | |
| The amount payable will decrease | ✓ |

## Test your learning

1   How long does HMRC usually require relevant VAT documents to be kept?

**Tick the relevant box below.**

|  | ✓ |
|---|---|
| 1 year |  |
| 2 years |  |
| 6 years |  |
| 20 years |  |

2   **Which TWO of the following statements about pro forma invoices are correct? Tick the relevant boxes below.**

|  | ✓ |
|---|---|
| A pro forma invoice is always sent out when goods are sent to customers, before issuing the proper invoice. |  |
| A pro forma invoice should always include the words 'This is not a VAT invoice'. |  |
| A customer can reclaim VAT stated on a pro forma invoice. |  |
| A pro forma invoice is sent out to offer a customer the chance to purchase the goods detailed. |  |

3   **In each of the following situations, state the tax point and whether this is a basic tax point or an actual tax point (B or A):**

|  | Date | Basic/Actual |
|---|---|---|
| An invoice is sent out to a customer for goods on 22 June 20X0 and the goods are despatched on 29 June 20X0. |  |  |
| Goods are sent out to a customer on 18 June 20X0 and this is followed by an invoice on 23 June 20X0. |  |  |
| A customer pays in full for goods on 27 June 20X0 and they are then delivered to the customer on 2 July 20X0. |  |  |

4   A VAT-registered business sends goods out to a customer on 15 May 20X0. The VAT invoice is then sent later and is dated 20 May 20X0. The customer paid the invoice on 20 June 20X0.

**What is the tax point for these goods?**

|  | ✓ |
|---|---|
| 15 May 20X0 | |
| 20 May 20X0 | |
| 20 June 20X0 | |

5   A VAT-registered business received an order with a 10% deposit from a customer on 2 June 20X0. The goods were sent out to the customer on 11 June 20X0. The VAT invoice for the full amount is dated 29 June 20X0. The customer paid the remaining 90% on 31 July 20X0.

**Identify ONE or TWO tax point(s) for these goods.**

|  | ✓ |
|---|---|
| 2 June 20X0 | |
| 11 June 20X0 | |
| 29 June 20X0 | |
| 31 July 20X0 | |

6   **State the conditions for the VAT on an irrecoverable (bad) debt to be reclaimed from HMRC.**

# The VAT return

5

## Learning outcomes

Having studied this chapter you will be able to:

| 2.3 | Calculate the VAT due to, or from, the relevant tax authority |
|-----|------------------------------------------------------------------|
|     | • Disallow VAT that is not recoverable |
| 2.5 | Complete and submit a VAT return and make any associated payment within the statutory limits |

## Assessment context

Task 6 of the exam will require you to calculate the amount of VAT which will be included in a number of boxes of the VAT return.

Task 7 of the exam will require you to complete a full VAT return using data extracted from the accounting records. Additional transactions may need to be considered as well.

## Qualification context

As a qualified accounting technician, you should be able to understand the impact that certain transactions have on VAT as a whole, as well as the VAT return.

## Business context

Every registered business in the United Kingdom must generate a VAT return using the records which have been produced as part of the normal workings of the business.

# Chapter overview

**VAT return**

**VAT control account**
- Collects all the VAT transactions within the business for a certain period

**VAT transactions**
- Irrecoverable VAT
- Books of Prime Entry
- Bad debt relief

**VAT period**
- Quarterly
- Monthly
- Annually

# 1 The VAT control account

As businesses collect VAT on behalf of HMRC, all VAT must be accounted for separately to the business's funds. This is done by maintaining a **VAT control account**.

VAT is normally owed to HMRC and so is usually a liability to the business. Credit entries into this account will increase the amount owed to HMRC, and debit entries will reduce the amount owed.

An example of the entries found in the VAT control account is shown below.

## VAT CONTROL ACCOUNT

| VAT deductible (input tax) | £ | VAT payable (output tax) | £ |
|---|---|---|---|
| VAT on purchases – from the purchases day book | 3,578.90 | VAT on sales – from the sales day book | 5,368.70 |
| VAT on purchases – from the cash payments book | 586.73 | VAT on sales – from the cash receipts book | 884.56 |
| | 4,165.63 | | 6,253.26 |
| VAT allowable on EU acquisitions | 211.78 | VAT due on EU acquisitions | 211.78 |
| | | Net understatement of output VAT on previous returns | 287.52 |
| Bad debt relief | 33.60 | Net overclaim of input VAT from previous returns | 104.56 |
| | | Fuel scale charge | 28.15 |
| | | | |
| VAT on credit notes to customers – sales returns day book | 69.80 | VAT on credit notes from suppliers – purchases returns day book | 49.70 |
| **Total tax deductible** | 4,480.81 | **Total tax payable** | 6,934.97 |
| | | **Less total tax deductible** | 4,480.81 |
| | | ***Payable to HMRC*** | 2,454.16 |

These double entries will have a direct link to the **VAT return** and therefore to the overall amount payable to/repayable by HMRC in the VAT period.

In the assessment, you will need to identify the impact that certain transactions have on VAT or specifically on the VAT account.

## Activity 1: Credit note – Impact on VAT

A credit note for taxable supplies is being processed.

**Required**

**What will the effect on VAT be?**

**Choose ONE answer.**

A    Input VAT will increase
B    Input VAT will decrease
C    Output VAT will increase
D    Output VAT will decrease

**Solution:**

## 1.1 Impacts on the VAT account

**Irrecoverable VAT**

We know that businesses will be unable to reclaim input VAT on certain purchases and expenses. In this case, the VAT is part of the cost to the business and is therefore charged to the statement of profit or loss, or included in the cost of an asset on the statement of financial position.

For example, the double entry for buying a car for £10,000 (exclusive of VAT), where the VAT of £2,000 is irrecoverable, would be:

DEBIT    Motor vehicles account    £12,000
CREDIT  Cash account               £12,000

## Activity 2: Irrecoverable VAT – Impact on accounts

You have the following extract from a manufacturing business's cash payments during the last month.

**Required**

**Select either Yes or No in the right-hand box to show whether the input VAT can be reclaimed on the next VAT return.**

| Description | £ net | £ VAT | £ Total | Reclaim input VAT? |
|---|---|---|---|---|
| Office supplies | 200.00 | 40.00 | 240.00 | **Yes/No** |
| Purchase of company car | 19,250.00 | 3850.00 | 23,100.00 | **Yes/No** |
| Computer | 550.00 | 110.00 | 660.00 | **Yes/No** |
| UK business entertainment | 1,000.00 | 200.00 | 1,200.00 | **Yes/No** |

**Solution:**

## 1.2 Bad debt relief

When a business recovers the output VAT from a bad debt, then this will impact the VAT account.

For example, the double entry for a standard-rated taxable supply of £5,000 (exclusive of VAT) which has become a bad debt is as follows:

To record the initial sale:

DEBIT     Trade receivables     £6,000
CREDIT   Sales     £5,000
CREDIT   VAT account     £1,000 – the business expects to collect the VAT from the customer and therefore records it as VAT owed to HMRC

To record the bad debt:

DEBIT     Bad debt expense     £6,000
CREDIT   Trade receivables     £6,000

To reclaim the VAT on the bad debt (after the conditions have been met):

DEBIT     VAT account     £1,000 – the business needs to get that VAT back, and therefore reduces the VAT owed to HMRC
CREDIT   Bad debt expense     £1,000

## 1.3 Books of prime entry

The VAT account is part of the accounting system. As such, the books of prime entry will be used to post journals to the VAT account.

### Activity 1: Books of prime entry – Impact on VAT account

Given below are some VAT figures taken from a business's books of prime entry:

**Required**

**Identify whether the entry in the VAT control account will be a debit or credit. Tick the relevant box.**

|  | Debit | Credit | £ |
|---|---|---|---|
| **VAT figures** | | | |
| From the sales day book | | | 8,750.00 |
| From the sales returns day book | | | 437.50 |
| From the purchases day book | | | 5,250.00 |
| From the purchases returns day book | | | 393.75 |
| From the cash receipts book | | | 1,514.45 |
| From the cash payments book | | | 837.55 |

# 2 VAT period

A VAT period is the length of time covered by each VAT return.

Most businesses have three month VAT periods and submit quarterly returns in line with their year end.

However, there are some alternatives:

(a) A business may be eligible for the annual accounting scheme (see later) whereby only one return per year needs to be submitted.

(b) Repayment traders (those who sell wholly or primarily zero-rated goods, so will be in a VAT repayment position) can apply to complete a monthly VAT return.

# 3 Clearing the VAT account

## Illustration 1: VAT account entries

In the following example, a trader has output tax due to HMRC from quarter one of £2,500. The trader pays this to clear the account before the entries for quarter two are added.

In quarter two, total output tax on sales is £3,550 and total input tax on purchases is £1,750. This results in a balance due to HMRC of £1,800.

These total amounts will be shown on the VAT return for quarter two, with the balance of £1,800 being shown as VAT payable.

### VAT ACCOUNT

| Date 20XX | Reference | Debit £ | Date 20XX | Reference | Credit £ |
|---|---|---|---|---|---|
| QTR 1 | VAT paid | 2,500.00 | QTR 1 | VAT payable | 2,500.00 |
| QTR 2 | Input tax on purchases | 1,750.00 | QTR 2 | Output tax on sales | 3,550.00 |
| | Balance c/d | 1,800.00 | | | |
| | **Total** | **6,050.00** | | **Total** | **6,050.00** |
| | | | QTR 2 | VAT payable | 1,800.00 |

## Activity 4: Correction of error

A trader has VAT payable to HMRC for the quarter ended 31.03.20X0 of £3,750 and VAT payable for the quarter ended 30.06.20X0 of £4,200. These are the correct amounts shown on the VAT returns.

The trader pays the VAT for the quarter ended 31.03.20X0, but enters it onto the wrong side of the VAT control account.

**Required**

**Identify the balance showing on the VAT control account before this error is adjusted.**

| | ✓ |
|---|---|
| £7,950 | |
| £11,700 | |

# 4 The VAT return

## 4.1 VAT return

The boxes on a VAT return which a trader must fill in are as follows.

**Box 1**  **VAT due in this period on sales and other outputs:**

- The total of the output VAT on sales (include credit and cash sales)
- Less the VAT on any credit notes issued
- Plus any fuel scale charges
- Plus adjustments for earlier period errors (see Chapter 7).

**Box 2**  The **VAT due on any acquisitions** from other EU countries.

**Box 3**  The total of boxes 1 and 2.

**Box 4**  **VAT reclaimed in this period on purchases and other inputs, including acquisitions from the EC:**

- The total of the input VAT on purchases and expenses (include credit and cash purchases)

- Less the VAT on any credit notes received

- Plus the VAT on any acquisitions from other EU countries

- Plus bad debt relief

- Plus adjustments for earlier period errors (see Chapter 7).

**Box 5**  **Net VAT to be paid to HM Revenue & Customs or reclaimed by you:**

- Deduct box 4 (input tax) from box 3 (output tax)

- If box 3 (output tax) > box 4 (input tax), then tax is payable to HMRC

- If box 4 (input tax) > box 3 (output tax), then tax is reclaimable from HMRC

Boxes 6–9 deal with sales and purchases before any VAT is added. Accounting records such as purchases day books, sales day books and journals will be needed to complete these figures. Note that boxes 6–9 are stated in whole pounds (ie no pence are needed).

**Box 6** **Total value of sales and all other outputs, excluding any VAT:**

This is the total of all sales, **less credit notes issued** excluding VAT. It includes:

- Standard-rated sales
- Zero-rated sales (including exports)
- Exempt sales
- Supplies to EU member countries (despatches)

**Box 7** **Total value of purchases and all other inputs, excluding any VAT:**

This is the total of all purchases and other expenses, **less credit notes received**, excluding VAT. It includes:

- Standard-rated supplies (including standard-rated imports)
- Zero-rated supplies (including zero-rated imports)
- Exempt supplies
- Acquisitions from EU member countries

**Box 8** **Total value of all supplies of goods and related costs, excluding any VAT, to other EC Member States:**

Note: this figure is also included in box 6.

For the purposes of this assessment, you should not include in box 8 the value of goods supplied to EU customers who are not VAT-registered.

**Box 9** **Total value of all acquisitions of goods and related costs, excluding any VAT, from other EC Member States:**

Note: this figure is also included in box 7.

(Related costs includes items such as freight costs and insurance for the goods.)

The **value** of the supply or acquisition of goods from other EU countries is shown on the VAT return separately. This is used to provide information on movements of taxable goods within the EU.

These details are provided in the AAT reference material available during the assessment.

Below is a copy of the format of the VAT return that you can expect to see in the computer-based assessment.

| VAT return for quarter ended | | £ |
|---|---|---|
| VAT due in this period on **sales** and other outputs | Box 1 | |
| VAT due in this period on **acquisitions** from other **EC Member States** | Box 2 | |
| Total VAT due (**the sum of boxes 1 and 2**) | Box 3 | |
| VAT reclaimed in this period on **purchases** and other inputs, including acquisitions from the EC | Box 4 | |
| Net VAT to be paid to HM Revenue & Customs or reclaimed by you (**Difference between boxes 3 and 4 – if box 4 is greater than box 3, use a minus sign**) | Box 5 | |
| Total value of **sales** and all other outputs excluding any VAT. **Include your box 8 figure. Whole pounds only** | Box 6 | |
| Total value of **purchases** and all other inputs excluding any VAT. **Include your box 9 figure. Whole pounds only** | Box 7 | |
| Total value of all **supplies** of goods and related costs, excluding any VAT, to other **EC Member States. Whole pounds only** | Box 8 | |
| Total value of all **acquisitions** of goods and related costs, excluding any VAT, from other **EC Member States. Whole pounds only** | Box 9 | |

Information for boxes 1–4 can usually be extracted from the VAT account.

### Illustration 2: Completing the VAT return

This illustration shows how the business and accounting records are likely to be presented to you in the assessment.

The relevant ledger accounts are shown below for the quarter ended 31.3.20XX.

## Sales and sales returns account

| Date 20XX | Reference | Debit £ | Date 20XX | Reference | Credit £ |
|---|---|---|---|---|---|
| 1.1-31.3 | Sales returns day book – UK sales | 2,374.00 | 1.1-31.3 | Sales day book – UK sales | 52,111.00 |
| | | | 1.1-31.3 | Sales day book – EU despatches | 9,700.00 |
| | | | 1.1-31.3 | Sales day book – exports | 4,259.00 |
| 31.3 | Balance c/d | 74,041.00 | 1.1-31.3 | Cash book – UK sales | 10,345.00 |
| | Total | 76,415.00 | | Total | 76,415.00 |

## Purchases and purchases returns account

| Date 20XX | Reference | Debit £ | Date 20XX | Reference | Credit £ |
|---|---|---|---|---|---|
| 1.1-31.3 | Purchases day book – UK purchases | 17,980.00 | 1.1-31.3 | Purchases returns day book – UK purchases | 1,020.00 |
| 1.1-31.3 | Purchases day book – EU acquisitions | 3,256.00 | | | |
| 1.1-31.3 | Purchases day book – zero-rated imports | 2,220.00 | 31.3 | Balance c/d | 22,436.00 |
| | Total | 23,456.00 | | Total | 23,456.00 |

**VAT account**

| Date 20XX | Reference | Debit £ | Date 20XX | Reference | Credit £ |
|---|---|---|---|---|---|
| 1.1-31.3 | Sales returns day book | 474.80 | 1.1-31.3 | Sales day book | 10,422.20 |
| 1.1-31.3 | Purchases day book | 3,596.00 | 1.1-31.3 | Cash book – UK sales | 2,069.00 |
| | | | 1.1-31.3 | Purchases returns day book – UK purchases | 204.00 |

The following journal entry has been made to reflect a bad debt that is to be recoverable this quarter.

| | Debit £ | Credit £ |
|---|---|---|
| Bad debts expense account (net amount) | 975.00 | |
| VAT account | 195.00 | |
| Sales ledger control account (gross amount) | | 1,170.00 |

In addition, you are told that a fuel scale charge of £28.83 applies for the private use of an employee's car and VAT on EU acquisitions is £651.20.

EU despatches are to VAT-registered customers.

# 5 How to complete the VAT return

Now to complete the boxes. Note that figures are shown in pounds and pence in boxes 1-5, with the figures being rounded down (if necessary) to pounds for boxes 6-9.

**Workings**

| | | £ |
|---|---|---|
| Box 1 | VAT on sales from the sales day book | 10,422.20 |
| | VAT on sales from the cash book | 2,069.00 |
| | Fuel scale charge | 28.83 |
| | Less: VAT on credit notes | (474.80) |
| | | 12,045.23 |

| | | £ |
|---|---|---|
| Box 2 | VAT due on EU acquisitions | 651.20 |
| Box 3 | Total of box 1 and box 2 £12,045.23 + £651.20 | 12,696.43 |
| Box 4 | VAT on purchases from purchases day book | 3,596.00 |
| | VAT on EU acquisitions | 651.20 |
| | Bad debt relief | 195.00 |
| | Less: VAT on credit notes from suppliers | (204.00) |
| | | 4,238.20 |
| Box 5 | Net VAT due box 3 minus box 4 | |
| | £12,696.43 – £4,238.20 | 8,458.23 |
| Box 6 | Standard-rated credit UK sales | 52,111.00 |
| | Less: Standard-rated credit notes | (2,374.00) |
| | Cash sales | 10,345.00 |
| | EU despatches | 9,700.00 |
| | Exports | 4,259.00 |
| | | 74,041 |
| Box 7 | Standard-rated credit purchases | 17,980.00 |
| | Less: Standard-rated credit notes | (1,020.00) |
| | EU acquisitions | 3,256.00 |
| | Imports | 2,220.00 |
| | | 22,436 |
| Box 8 | EU sales | 9,700 |
| Box 9 | EU acquisitions | 3,256 |

| VAT return for quarter ended 31.3.20XX | | £ |
|---|---|---|
| VAT due in this period on **sales** and other outputs | Box 1 | 12,045.23 |
| VAT due in this period on **acquisitions** from other **EC Member States** | Box 2 | 651.20 |
| Total VAT due (**the sum of boxes 1 and 2**) | Box 3 | 12,696.43 |

| VAT return for quarter ended 31.3.20XX | | £ |
|---|---|---|
| VAT reclaimed in this period on **purchases** and other inputs, including acquisitions from the EC | Box 4 | 4,238.20 |
| Net VAT to be paid to HM Revenue & Customs or reclaimed by you (**Difference between boxes 3 and 4 – if box 4 is greater than box 3, use a minus sign**) | Box 5 | 8,458.23 |
| Total value of **sales** and all other outputs excluding any VAT. **Include your box 8 figure. Whole pounds only** | Box 6 | 74,041 |
| Total value of **purchases** and all other inputs excluding any VAT. **Include your box 9 figure. Whole pounds only** | Box 7 | 22,436 |
| Total value of all **supplies** of goods and related costs, excluding any VAT, to other **EC Member States. Whole pounds only** | Box 8 | 9,700 |
| Total value of all **acquisitions** of goods and related costs, excluding any VAT, from other **EC Member States. Whole pounds only** | Box 9 | 3,256 |

## Activity 5: David Ltd – VAT return

### VAT exercise

The following details have been extracted from the daybooks of David Ltd.

### Sales: UK

| Date | | Debit £ | Credit £ |
|---|---|---|---|
| 31/10/X2 | Sales day book | | 20,629.77 |
| 30/11/X2 | Sales day book | | 23,673.85 |
| 31/12/X2 | Sales day book | | 25,497.42 |

### Sales: EU despatches

| Date | | Debit £ | Credit £ |
|---|---|---|---|
| 31/10/X2 | Sales day book | | 2,292.10 |
| 30/11/X2 | Sales day book | | 2,406.72 |
| 31/12/X2 | Sales day book | | 2,502.99 |

## Purchases: UK

| Date | | Debit £ | Credit £ |
|------|--|---------|----------|
| 31/10/X2 | Purchases day book | 14,231.10 | |
| 30/11/X2 | Purchases day book | 15,962.63 | |
| 31/12/X2 | Purchases day book | 16,436.91 | |

## VAT: Output tax

| Date | | Debit £ | Credit £ |
|------|--|---------|----------|
| 31/10/X2 | Sales day book | | 4,125.95 |
| 30/11/X2 | Sales day book | | 4,734.77 |
| 31/12/X2 | Sales day book | | 5,099.84 |

## VAT: Input tax

| Date | | Debit £ | Credit £ |
|------|--|---------|----------|
| 31/10/X2 | Purchases day book | 2,846.22 | |
| 30/11/X2 | Purchases day book | 3,192.52 | |
| 31/12/X2 | Purchases day book | 3,287.38 | |

- Bad debt relief on a sales invoice for £85.41 including VAT is to be claimed in this quarter.
- VAT returns are completed online quarterly.
- VAT payable or receivable is settled by electronic bank transfer.
- Today's date is 15/01/X3.

**Required**

(a) **Calculate and insert the figure to be reclaimed for bad debt relief.**

£ [        ]

**(b)** **Complete boxes 1 to 9 of the VAT return for the quarter ended 31 December X2.**

| Box 1 | VAT due in this period on **sales** and other outputs | |
|---|---|---|
| Box 2 | VAT due in this period on **acquisitions** from other **EC Member States** | |
| Box 3 | Total VAT due (**the sum of boxes 1 and 2**) | |
| Box 4 | VAT reclaimed in the period on **purchases** and other inputs, including acquisitions from the EC | |
| Box 5 | Net VAT to be paid to HM Revenue & Customs or reclaimed by you. (**Difference between boxes 3 and 4**) | |
| Box 6 | Total value of **sales** and all other outputs excluding any VAT. **Include your box 8 figure. Whole pounds only.** | |
| Box 7 | Total value of purchases and all other inputs excluding any VAT. **Include your box 9 figure. Whole pounds only.** | |
| Box 8 | Total value of all **supplies** of goods and related costs, excluding any VAT, to other **EC Member States. Whole pounds only.** | |
| Box 9 | Total value of all **acquisitions** of goods and related costs, excluding any VAT, from other **EC Member States. Whole pounds only.** | |

**Solution:**

## Submission deadlines

It is mandatory for most VAT-registered traders to submit their returns online and pay electronically.

In this case, their submission and payment will be due seven calendar days after the end of the month following the end of the return period.

For example, the submission and payment date for the quarter ended 31 March will be 7 May.

The exceptions to this rule are as follows:

(a) Traders who are eligible for the annual accounting scheme (see later).

(b) Traders who are still able to submit paper returns. For them, the submission date is one month after the end of the VAT period.

(c) Traders who make payments on account (see later). For them, the submission date is one month after the end of the VAT period.

(d) Traders who pay by direct debit. These businesses will receive an extra three days on top of the normal submission date to make the payment.

This information is in the AAT reference material available in your assessment.

## Chapter summary

- The VAT account records the VAT payable and reclaimable by the business and is a link between the business records and the VAT return.

- Normally every quarter the VAT return must be completed and submitted to HMRC, together with any payment by the due date.

- The first five boxes of the VAT return can usually be completed from the figures in the VAT account.

- Boxes 6 to 9 must be completed from the other accounting records of the business showing sales and purchases, despatches and acquisitions excluding VAT.

- The VAT return is generally due one month and seven days following the end of the relevant VAT return period.

## Keywords

- **VAT (control) account:** the ledger account in which all amounts of input tax and output tax are recorded

- **VAT return:** the form which must be completed and submitted to HMRC to show the amount of VAT due or to be reclaimed, usually for the quarter

## Activity 1: Credit note – Impact on VAT

D    Output VAT will decrease. When the original supply was made, output VAT would have been recorded. A credit note is now having the effect of reversing that sale, so the output VAT needs to be reversed down again.

## Activity 2: Irrecoverable VAT – Impact on accounts

| Description | £ net | £ VAT | £ Total | Reclaim input VAT? |
|---|---|---|---|---|
| Office supplies | 200.00 | 40.00 | 240.00 | **Yes** |
| Purchase of company car | 19,250.00 | 3850.00 | 23,100.00 | **No** |
| Computer | 550.00 | 110.00 | 660.00 | **Yes** |
| UK business entertainment | 1,000.00 | 200.00 | 1,200.00 | **No** |

## Activity 3: Books of prime entry – Impact on VAT account

| | Debit | Credit | £ |
|---|---|---|---|
| **VAT figures** | | | |
| From the sales day book | | ✓ | 8,750.00 |
| From the sales returns day book | ✓ | | 437.50 |
| From the purchases day book | ✓ | | 5,250.00 |
| From the purchases returns day book | | ✓ | 393.75 |
| From the cash receipts book | | ✓ | 1,514.45 |
| From the cash payments book | ✓ | | 837.55 |

## Activity 4: Correction of errors

|  | ✓ |
|---|---|
| £7,950 | |
| £11,700 | ✓ |

By entering the VAT paid debit of £3,750.00, on the credit side, the balance on the account is showing as £11,700 instead of the correct £4,200.00

| Date 20X0 | Reference | Debit £ | Date 20X0 | Reference | Credit £ |
|---|---|---|---|---|---|
| | | | 31/3/X0 | VAT payable | 3,750.00 |
| | VAT paid should be here! | VAT paid should be here! | **31/3/X0** | **VAT paid** | **3,750.00** |
| | | | 30/6/X0 | VAT payable | 4,200.00 |
| | Balance | 11,700.00 | | | |
| | **Total** | **11,700.00** | | **Total** | **11,700.00** |
| | | | | | |

## Activity 5: David Ltd – VAT return

(a)　£14.23 (W) (note: this figure to be added to Box 4)

(b)

| Box 1 | VAT due in this period on **sales** and other outputs | 13,960.56 |
|---|---|---|
| Box 2 | VAT due in this period on **acquisitions** from other **EC Member States** | 0.00 |
| Box 3 | Total VAT due (**the sum of boxes 1 and 2**) | 13,960.56 |
| Box 4 | VAT reclaimed in the period on **purchases** and other inputs, including acquisitions from the EC | 9,340.35 (W) |
| Box 5 | Net VAT to be paid to HM Revenue & Customs or reclaimed by you (**Difference between boxes 3 and 4**) | 4,620.21 |
| Box 6 | Total value of **sales** and all other outputs excluding any VAT. **Include your box 8 figure** | 77,002 |

| Box 7 | Total value of purchases and all other inputs excluding any VAT. **Include your box 9 figure** | 46,630 |
| Box 8 | Total value of all **supplies** of goods and related costs, excluding any VAT, to other **EC Member States** | 7,201 |
| Box 9 | Total value of all **acquisitions** of goods and related costs, excluding any VAT, from other **EC Member States** | 0 |

| (W) | £ |
| --- | --- |
| VAT on purchases | 9,326.12 |
| VAT on bad debt = £85.41 × $\frac{1}{6}$ | 14.23 |
| | 9,340.35 |

BPP
LEARNING MEDIA

## Test your learning

1   **Decide whether the following statements are true or false. Tick the relevant boxes below.**

| | True ✓ | False ✓ |
|---|---|---|
| If input VAT is greater than output VAT on the return, VAT is payable to HMRC. | | |
| If output VAT is greater than input VAT on the return, VAT is repayable from HMRC. | | |

2   Holly completed her VAT return for the latest quarter. It correctly indicates that she owes HMRC £7,520 VAT. However, her VAT account is showing an amount due of £12,220. VAT payable for the previous quarter was £4,700.

**Tick which ONE of the following statements explains the difference:**

| | ✓ |
|---|---|
| The payment of £4,700 for the previous quarter has been included twice in the VAT account. | |
| The payment of £4,700 for the previous quarter has been omitted from the VAT account. | |

3   The ledger accounts of a VAT-registered trader for the quarter ended 30.6.20XX are shown below:

**Sales and sales returns account**

| Date 20XX | Reference | Debit £ | Date 20XX | Reference | Credit £ |
|---|---|---|---|---|---|
| 1.4-30.6 | Sales returns day book – UK sales | 2,400.00 | 1.4-30.6 | Sales day book – UK sales | 26,000.00 |
| | | | 1.4-30.6 | Sales day book – exports | 5,800.00 |
| 30.6 | Balance c/d | 43,400.00 | 1.4-30.6 | Cash book – UK sales | 14,000.00 |
| | **Total** | **45,800.00** | | **Total** | **45,800.00** |

## Purchases account

| Date 20XX | Reference | Debit £ | Date 20XX | Reference | Credit £ |
|---|---|---|---|---|---|
| 1.4-30.6 | Purchases day book – UK purchases | 15,500.00 | | | |
| 1.4-30.6 | Purchases day book – EU acquisitions | 3,750.00 | 30.6 | Balance c/d | 19,250.00 |
| | **Total** | **19,250.00** | | **Total** | **19,250.00** |

## VAT account

| Date 20XX | Reference | Debit £ | Date 20XX | Reference | Credit £ |
|---|---|---|---|---|---|
| 1.4-30.6 | Sales returns day book | 480.00 | 1.4-30.6 | Sales day book | 5,200.00 |
| 1.4-30.6 | Purchases day book | 3,100.00 | 1.4-30.6 | Cash book – UK sales | 2,800.00 |
| | | | | | |
| | | | | | |

In addition, you are told that bad debt relief on a sales invoice of £500.00 excluding VAT is to be claimed this quarter.

VAT on EU acquisitions is £750.00.

**Complete boxes 1 to 9 of the VAT return below for the quarter ended 30.6.20XX.**

| VAT return for quarter ended 30.6.20XX | | £ |
|---|---|---|
| VAT due in this period on **sales** and other outputs | Box 1 | |
| VAT due in this period on **acquisitions** from other **EC Member States** | Box 2 | |
| Total VAT due (**the sum of boxes 1 and 2**) | Box 3 | |
| VAT reclaimed in this period on **purchases** and other inputs, including acquisitions from the EC | Box 4 | |

| VAT return for quarter ended 30.6.20XX | | £ |
|---|---|---|
| Net VAT to be paid to HM Revenue & Customs or reclaimed by you **(Difference between boxes 3 and 4 – if box 4 is greater than box 3, use a minus sign)** | Box 5 | |
| Total value of **sales** and all other outputs, excluding any VAT. **Include your box 8 figure. Whole pounds only** | Box 6 | |
| Total value of **purchases** and all other inputs, excluding any VAT. **Include your box 9 figure. Whole pounds only** | Box 7 | |
| Total value of all **supplies** of goods and related costs, excluding any VAT, to other **EC Member States. Whole pounds only** | Box 8 | |
| Total value of all **acquisitions** of goods and related costs, excluding any VAT, from other **EC Member States. Whole pounds only** | Box 9 | |

4   The following ledger accounts are shown below of a VAT-registered trader for quarter ended 31 May 20XX.

**Sales and sales returns account**

| Date 20XX | Reference | Debit £ | Date 20XX | Reference | Credit £ |
|---|---|---|---|---|---|
| 1.3-31.5 | Sales returns day book – UK standard-rated sales | 398.86 | 1.3-31.5 | Sales day book – UK standard-rated sales | 30,678.25 |
| 1.3-31.5 | Sales returns day book – UK zero-rated sales | 25.59 | 1.3-31.5 | Sales day book – UK zero-rated sales | 3,581.67 |
| 31.5 | Balance c/d | 38,890.28 | 1.3-31.5 | Cash book - UK standard-rated sales | 5,054.51 |
| | **Total** | **39,314.43** | | **Total** | **39,314.43** |

## Purchases account

| Date 20XX | Reference | Debit £ | Date 20XX | Reference | Credit £ |
|---|---|---|---|---|---|
| 1.3-31.5 | Purchases day book – UK standard-rated purchases | 20,450.85 | | | |
| 1.3-31.5 | Purchases day book – UK zero-rated purchases | 2,669.80 | | | |
| 1.3-31.5 | Cash book – UK standard-rated purchases/ expenses | 3,033.01 | 31.5 | Balance c/d | 26,153.66 |
| | **Total** | **26,153.66** | | **Total** | **26,153.66** |

## VAT account

| Date 20XX | Reference | Debit £ | Date 20XX | Reference | Credit £ |
|---|---|---|---|---|---|
| 1.3-31.5 | Sales returns day book | 79.77 | 1.3-31.5 | Sales day book | 6,135.65 |
| 1.3-31.5 | Purchases day book | 4,090.17 | 1.3-31.5 | Cash book | 1,010.90 |
| 1.3-31.5 | Cash book | 606.60 | | | |

## Journal (extract)

| | Debit £ | Credit £ |
|---|---|---|
| Irrecoverable (bad) debts expense | 192.00 | |
| VAT account | 38.40 | |
| Receivables (debtors) (VAT inclusive at 20%) | | 230.40 |

**Complete boxes 1 to 9 of the VAT return for quarter ended 31 May 20XX**

| VAT return for quarter ended | | £ |
|---|---|---|
| VAT due in this period on **sales** and other outputs | Box 1 | |
| VAT due in this period on **acquisitions** from other **EC Member States** | Box 2 | |
| Total VAT due (**the sum of boxes 1 and 2)** | Box 3 | |
| VAT reclaimed in this period on **purchases** and other inputs, including acquisitions from the EC | Box 4 | |
| Net VAT to be paid to HM Revenue & Customs or reclaimed by you (**Difference between boxes 3 and 4 – if box 4 is greater than box 3, use a minus sign)** | Box 5 | |
| Total value of **sales** and all other outputs, excluding any VAT. **Include your box 8 figure. Whole pounds only** | Box 6 | |
| Total value of **purchases** and all other inputs excluding any VAT. **Include your box 9 figure. Whole pounds only** | Box 7 | |
| Total value of all **supplies** of goods and related costs, excluding any VAT, to other **EC Member States. Whole pounds only** | Box 8 | |
| Total value of all **acquisitions** of goods and related costs, excluding any VAT, from other **EC Member States. Whole pounds only** | Box 9 | |

5    **Identify which ONE of the following statements in relation to acquisition of goods from other EU countries and how they are dealt with on the VAT return is correct.**

| | ✓ |
|---|---|
| Input tax paid at the ports is reclaimed as input tax on the VAT return. | |
| Both input tax and output tax in relation to the goods are shown on the VAT return. | |
| They are zero-rated and so no VAT features on the VAT return. | |
| They are exempt and so no VAT features on the VAT return. | |

6 **Identify which of the following statement(s) is/are correct. There may be more than one correct statement.**

| | ✓ |
|---|---|
| The fuel scale charge increases output VAT and is shown in box 1. | |
| VAT on EU acquisitions increases both input VAT and output VAT and is shown in boxes 1 and 4. | |
| Credit notes received from suppliers reduce input VAT and are shown in box 4. | |
| Credit notes issued to customers reduce output VAT and are shown in box 1. | |

7 Vincent is VAT-registered and sells standard-rated items both in the UK and overseas. Sales (excluding VAT) for the quarter ended 31.3.X0 are split as follows:

- UK sales – £27,200.00
- Exports (outside EU) – £9,705.00
- Despatches (within EU) to VAT-registered customers – £18,345.00
- Despatches (within EU) to non-VAT-registered customers – £7,200.00

**Complete the following extract of the VAT return**

| VAT return for quarter ended 31.03.20X0 | | £ |
|---|---|---|
| VAT due in this period on **sales** and other outputs | Box 1 | |
| Total value of **sales** and all other outputs, excluding any VAT. **Include your box 8 figure. Whole pounds only** | Box 6 | |
| Total value of all **supplies** of goods and related costs, excluding any VAT, to other **EC Member States. Whole pounds only** | Box 8 | |

8 Valerie is VAT-registered and purchases standard-rated items for her business, both in the UK and overseas. Purchases (excluding VAT) for the quarter ended 31.3.X0 are split as follows:

- UK purchases – £9,230.00
- Imports (outside EU) – £1,205.00
- Acquisitions (within EU) from VAT-registered suppliers – £8,345.00

## Complete the following extract of the VAT return

| VAT return for quarter ended 31.03.20X0 | | £ |
|---|---|---|
| VAT due in this period on **acquisitions** from other **EC Member States** | Box 2 | |
| VAT reclaimed in the period on **purchases** and other inputs, including acquisitions from the EC | Box 4 | |
| Total value of purchases and all other inputs, excluding any VAT. **Include your box 9 figure. Whole pounds only** | Box 7 | |
| Total value of all **acquisitions** of goods and related costs, excluding any VAT, from other **EC Member States. Whole pounds only** | Box 9 | |

# VAT schemes for small businesses

## Learning outcomes

| 1.3 | Explain, for these VAT schemes: annual accounting; cash accounting; flat-rate scheme; standard scheme: |
|---|---|
| | • The thresholds and qualification criteria for the special VAT schemes |
| | • Why being in the normal VAT scheme or in one or more of the special VAT schemes affect the timing and frequency of filing returns and payment of VAT |

## Assessment context

Task 3 will ask you questions in respect of the schemes. Details of VAT schemes will be provided in the reference material onscreen in the exam.

## Qualification context

As an accounting technician, you will need to have an appreciation of schemes available for small businesses. You will not need to know the schemes in great detail but will need to be able to talk about them at a basic level.

## Business context

Knowing what options are available to a business in respect of registering for VAT is important as there are schemes which can help cut down the cost of administration.

# Chapter overview

**VAT schemes**

| Standard scheme | Cash accounting scheme | Annual accounting scheme | Flat rate scheme |
| --- | --- | --- | --- |
| • Quarterly return | • Quarterly return | • Annual return | • Quarterly return |
| • Payment due one month and seven days after the VAT period if made electronically | • VAT accounted for when cash received/paid | • Nine instalments due within the year | • Simplified VAT payable calculation |
| | | • Balance due two months after the year end | |

# 1 Schemes

When registering for VAT, there are several schemes that a business may be eligible to opt for. In the exam, you will be required to be able to explain whether a business is eligible for each scheme. The four schemes on your syllabus are:

1    The standard scheme
2    The cash accounting scheme
3    The annual accounting scheme
4    The flat-rate scheme.

# 2 The standard scheme

This is the scheme that a business is automatically entered into when it registers for VAT.

- VAT returns are completed on a quarterly basis.

- Repayment traders (for example, zero-rated suppliers) may opt to complete a VAT return each month.

- Payments are made one month and seven days from the end of the VAT period if the submission is electronic. This is reduced to one month from the end of the VAT period if it is a paper submission.

# 3 The cash accounting scheme

The **cash accounting scheme** enables businesses to ignore the tax point rules and account for VAT only when it is paid and received.

## 3.1 Conditions

- The scheme can only be used when a business's VAT-exclusive taxable turnover is not expected to exceed £1,350,000 in the next 12 months.

- Businesses will only be eligible if they are not a member of the flat rate scheme (see later).

- A taxable person can join the scheme only if all returns and VAT payments are up to date (or arrangements have been made to pay outstanding VAT by instalments).

- The taxable person must also not have been convicted of a VAT offence or penalty in the previous 12 months.

- Once in the scheme, if VAT-exclusive taxable supplies exceed £1,600,000 in the previous 12 months or next 12 months (estimated), notice must be given to HM Revenue & Customs (HMRC) within 30 days and the business must exit the cash accounting scheme (they may be able to use the scheme for a further 6 months).

## 3.2 Return and payment submission dates

The due dates are the same as for the standard scheme, unless the business has also entered into the annual accounting scheme.

## 3.3 Advantages

Output VAT is not paid to HMRC until it has been collected from the customer, leading to a cashflow advantage over the standard scheme. This is especially beneficial if the business offers long credit terms to customers, but pays its suppliers promptly.

Cash accounting gives automatic bad debt relief as the output VAT is only paid over to HMRC when it is received from the customer.

## Activity 1: Julie Ltd – Cash accounting scheme

Julie Ltd receives cash for most of its sales, buys most of its purchases on credit and has an estimated turnover for the next 12 months of £1,200,000.

**Required**

**(a)** **What is the turnover limit for ceasing to use the cash accounting scheme? Choose ONE answer.**

A    Estimated turnover in the next 12 months is more than £1,350,000
B    Estimated turnover in the next 12 months is more than £1,600,000

**(b)** **Is the business eligible to join the cash accounting scheme? Choose ONE answer.**

A    Yes
B    No

# 4 The annual accounting scheme

The **annual accounting scheme** allows businesses to submit only one VAT return each year. They are still, however, required to make payments throughout the year.

## 4.1 Return and payment submission dates

The trader pays 90% of the prior year VAT liability (or of an estimate if this is the business's first year of trading), in 9 equal instalments over months 4 to 12 of the year.

The remaining balance is settled 2 months after the year end and submitted with the VAT return form.

Month 1

End of
Month 4

9 × monthly payments = 1/10 of
previous year's liability

End of
Month 14

Submit return and
final payment

## 4.2 Conditions

- VAT-exclusive taxable turnover is not expected to exceed £1,350,000 in the next 12 months.

- All returns and VAT payments are up to date (or arrangements have been made to pay outstanding VAT by instalments).

- Once registered with the scheme, if VAT-exclusive taxable supplies exceed £1,600,000 in the previous 12 months, notice must be given to HMRC within 30 days and the business must leave the scheme.

## 4.3 Advantages of the annual accounting scheme

- Submitting only one VAT return reduces the administrative burden of VAT.

- The business has an extra month between the end of the VAT period and the return submission date.

- Paying a fixed amount on each instalment makes cashflow management easier.

## 4.4 Disadvantages of the annual accounting scheme

- If turnover decreases, the interim payments may be higher than they need to be.

- The business will have to wait until the end of the year when it submits its return for a refund.

### Activity 2: Thelma Ray – Annual accounting scheme

**Using the picklist over the page, complete the following email to a client who has had a small business for many years.**

To:      Thelma Ray
From:   AN Accountant
Date:   15 October
Subject: Annual Accounting Scheme

Dear Thelma Ray,

Please be advised that based on your VAT liability for last year of £90,000, and the fact that your VAT year ends on 30 September, your payments for the next VAT year will be as follows:

**Payments on Account**

[ ▼ ] will be payable at the end of each month for [ ▼ ] months. The first payment will be due in [ ▼ ] .

**Balancing Payment**

The balancing payment and annual return will be due at the end of [ ▼ ] . [ ▼ ] will be payable if you expect your liability to increase by £12,000 next year.

Kind regards

AN Accountant

**Picklists:**

| (1) | £9,000 | £10,000 | £7,500 |
|-----|--------|---------|--------|
| (2) | 12 | 6 | 9 |
| (3) | January | March | October |
| (4) | March | November | September |
| (5) | £9,000 | £12,000 | £21,000 |

# 5 Flat-rate scheme

The **flat rate scheme** makes the calculation of the VAT liability simpler, by calculating the amount of VAT payable as a flat (industry-specific) percentage of total VAT-inclusive turnover.

## 5.1 Conditions

- A business's **VAT-exclusive** taxable turnover is not expected to exceed £150,000 in the next 12 months.

- The business is not a member of the cash accounting scheme.

- If **VAT-inclusive** taxable supplies exceed £230,000 in the previous 12 months, notice must be given to HMRC within 30 days and the business must leave the scheme.

## 5.2 Return and payment submission dates

The due dates are the same as for the standard scheme, unless the business has also entered into the annual accounting scheme.

The VAT payable is calculated in a completely different way than usual, by applying a flat rate percentage to the total VAT-inclusive turnover of all supplies, so no input VAT is reclaimable.

Output VAT is charged as normal to customers.

## 5.3 Advantages of the flat rate scheme

- VAT payable is normally less than the amount payable under the standard accounting scheme.
- There will be simplified administration as VAT does not have to be accounted for on each individual sales and purchase invoice.
- Cash flow can be managed as the VAT payable is a percentage of turnover.

## Activity 3: Phyllis – Flat rate scheme

Phyllis, making only standard-rated supplies, wants to join the flat rate scheme.

The flat rate percentage applied to her business sector is 8%.

The VAT-exclusive turnover for the quarter is £40,000.

Phyllis also made purchases of £20,000, inclusive of standard rate VAT.

**Required**

**(a) If Phyllis opted for the flat rate scheme, what would be the VAT payable for the quarter?**

**(b) If Phyllis didn't opt for the flat rate scheme, what would be the VAT payable for the quarter? (to the nearest £1)**

**Solution:**

## Chapter summary

- If a VAT-registered business has an annual VAT-exclusive turnover of no more than £1,350,000, it may be eligible for the annual accounting scheme – under which nine monthly direct debit payments are made, usually based upon the previous year's VAT liability. The balancing payment is made when the VAT return for the year is submitted within two months of the year end.

- If a VAT-registered business has an annual VAT-exclusive turnover of no more than £1,350,000, it may be eligible for the cash accounting scheme – under which VAT has to be accounted for to HMRC on the basis of cash payments received and made, rather than under the normal tax point rules.

- If a VAT-registered business has an annual VAT-exclusive turnover of no more than £150,000, it may be eligible for the flat rate scheme – under which it can simplify its VAT records by calculating its VAT payment as a percentage of total (VAT-inclusive) turnover instead of recording the input and output tax on each individual purchase and sales invoice.

## Keywords

- **Annual accounting scheme:** a method of accounting for VAT which does not require quarterly returns and payments – instead, it requires nine monthly direct debit payments and one annual return, accompanied by the final balancing payment

- **Cash accounting scheme:** a method of accounting for VAT which allows VAT to be dealt with according to the date of payment or receipt of cash, rather than under the normal tax point rules

- **Flat rate scheme:** enables businesses to calculate their VAT payment as a percentage of total VAT-inclusive turnover

## Activity 1: Julie Ltd – Cash accounting scheme

(a)  B    Estimated turnover in the next 12 months is more than £1,600,000

(b)  A    Yes

## Activity 2: Thelma Ray – Annual accounting scheme

To:      Thelma Ray
From:   AN Accountant
Date:    15 October
Subject: Annual Accounting Scheme

Dear Thelma Ray,

Please be advised that based on your VAT liability for last year, £90,000, and that your VAT year ends on 30 September, your payments for the next VAT year will be as follows:

**Payments on Account**

| **£9,000** | will be payable at the end of each month for | **9** | months. The first

payment will be due in | **January** |.

**Balancing Payment**

The balancing payment and annual return will be due at the end of | **November** |.

| **£21,000** | **(Working)** will be payable if you expect your liability to increase by £12,000 next year.

Kind regards

AN Accountant

**Working**

VAT liability for the year: £81,000 + £12,000 = £102,000

| Less: (£90,000/10) × 9 = | (£81,000) |
| Balancing payment | £21,000 |

# Activity 3: Phyllis – Flat rate scheme

(a)  VAT-Inclusive Turnover: £40,000 x 120% = £48,000

VAT Payable: £48,000 × 8% = £3,840

(b)  Output VAT:          £40,000 × 20%    £8,000

Input VAT:            £20,000 × $\dfrac{20}{120}$     (£3,333)

Total VAT Payable                        £4,667

1 **Using the picklist below, complete the following letter concerning the Annual Accounting Scheme to Jacob Lymstock, a client of yours who has had a small business for several years.**

AN accountant
Number Street
London
SW11 8AB

Mr Lymstock
Alphabet Street
London
W12 6WM

Dear Mr Lymstock

ANNUAL ACCOUNTING SCHEME

I have recently been reviewing your files. I would like to make you aware of a scheme that you could use for VAT.

As the annual value of your taxable supplies, [_____ ▼] (1) VAT and supplies of capital items, in the following 12 months is expected to be [_____ ▼] (2) [_____ ▼] (3) you can join the annual accounting scheme.

Under this scheme, you make [_____ ▼] (4) monthly direct debit payments based on your VAT liability for the previous year. The first of these payments is due at the end of the [_____ ▼] (5) month of the accounting period. You must then prepare a VAT return for the year and submit it with the balancing payment, by [_____ ▼] (6) after the year end.

Use of this annual accounting scheme is a great help, as it means that you only have to prepare [_____ ▼] (7) VAT return(s) each year.

If you wish to discuss this with me in more detail, please do not hesitate to contact me.

Yours sincerely

AN Accountant

**Picklists:**

(1) including/excluding
(2) no more than/greater than
(3) £1,350,000/£1,600,000
(4) 4/9/10/12

(5)   first/fourth/twelfth

(6)   30 days/one month/two months

(7)   one/four/12

2   **Complete the following statements about the Cash Accounting Scheme using the picklists below.**

If the annual value of taxable supplies, [          ] (1) VAT, is [          ] (2) than [          ] (3) and provided that a trader has a clean record with HMRC, he may be able to apply to use the cash accounting scheme.

The scheme allows the accounting for VAT to be based upon the date of [          ] (4). This is particularly useful for a business which gives its customers a [          ] (5) period of credit whilst paying its suppliers promptly.

The scheme also gives automatic relief [          ] (6) so if the customer does not pay the amount due, then the VAT need not be accounted for to HMRC.

### Picklists:

(1)   including/excluding

(2)   no more/greater

(3)   £1,350,000/£1,600,000

(4)   receipt and payment of money/invoice

(5)   long/short

(6)   from filing VAT returns/for bad debts

3   An existing trader makes standard-rated supplies and uses the flat rate scheme. The flat rate percentage that he must use is 11.5%.

For the quarter ended 31 Mar 20X0, the trader had total turnover of £9,500 excluding VAT. He also had VAT-exclusive purchases of £3,000.

(a)   **Which figure reflects the amount of VAT payable to HMRC? Tick the box with the correct answer.**

|  | ✓ |
|---|---|
| £897.00 |  |
| £1,092.50 |  |
| £1,311.00 |  |

(b)   **In this quarter, would the trader have more or less VAT to pay to HMRC if he was not in the flat rate scheme? Tick the box with the correct answer.**

|  | ✓ |
|---|---|
| More VAT is payable not using the flat rate scheme |  |
| More VAT is payable using the flat rate scheme |  |

4   A trader has joined the annual accounting scheme for the year ended 31 December 2016.

**Identify whether the following statement is true or false.**

|  | True ✓ | False ✓ |
|---|---|---|
| The first payment due to HMRC is by 1 April 2016. |  |  |

5   **Would the cash accounting scheme improve the cash flow of a retail business that receives most of its sales in cash and buys most of its purchases on credit? Tick ONE of the boxes.**

|  | ✓ |
|---|---|
| Yes, because they would be able to reclaim input VAT earlier |  |
| Yes, because they would pay output VAT later |  |
| No, because they would reclaim input VAT later |  |
| No, because they would pay output VAT earlier |  |

6   A trader, making standard-rated (20%) supplies, has joined the flat rate scheme.

The flat rate percentage applying to his business sector is 8.5%.

His VAT-exclusive turnover for the quarter is £30,000.

**What is the VAT due to HMRC for the quarter?**

|  | ✓ |
|---|---|
| £2,550 |  |
| £3,060 |  |

# Administration

7

## Learning outcomes

Having studied this chapter you will be able to:

| | |
|---|---|
| **1.1** | Identify and analyse relevant information on VAT<br>Demonstrating an understanding of:<br><ul><li>Relevant sources of VAT information needed by a business</li><li>How to analyse available information and identify relevant items to extract</li><li>How to communicate relevant regulatory information to others within the business</li><li>The ethical and legal implications of failure to identify and apply information and regulations to the business</li></ul> |
| **1.2** | Explain the necessary interaction with the relevant tax authority regarding:<br><ul><li>Their power to require businesses to comply with regulations about registration, record keeping, submissions of VAT returns and payment of VAT due</li><li>How and when it is appropriate to obtain guidance from the relevant tax authority about VAT matters, particularly in respect of issues where there is doubt over the correct treatment</li><li>Their rights in respect of inspection of records and control visits</li></ul> |
| **1.5** | Maintain knowledge of legislation, regulation, guidance and codes of practice |
| **2.4** | Make adjustments and declarations for any errors or omissions identified in previous VAT periods |
| **3.1** | Explain the implications for a business of failure to comply with registration requirements |
| **3.2** | Explain the implications for a business of failure to comply with the requirement to submit VAT returns |
| **3.3** | Explain the implications for a business of failure to comply with the requirement to make payment of VAT |
| **4.1** | Inform the appropriate person about VAT-related matters |
| **4.2** | Communicate information about VAT due to or from the tax authority |

# Assessment context

Task 4 may ask for information in respect of errors and penalties which relate to the VAT system. There is a lot of information within the reference material which is available in the assessment.

Task 8 will require you to complete a communication to either a client or HMRC using pick lists.

# Qualification context

As an accounting technician, you will need to be aware of the consequences of not completing VAT returns accurately or on time. You will also need to know how to communicate with clients or HMRC formally.

# Business context

If tasks are not completed within a finance role, then there is a risk of the business being subject to penalties. It is important to know these consequences.

Formal communication will also be required for both internal and external communication and it is a skill which requires practise.

# Chapter overview

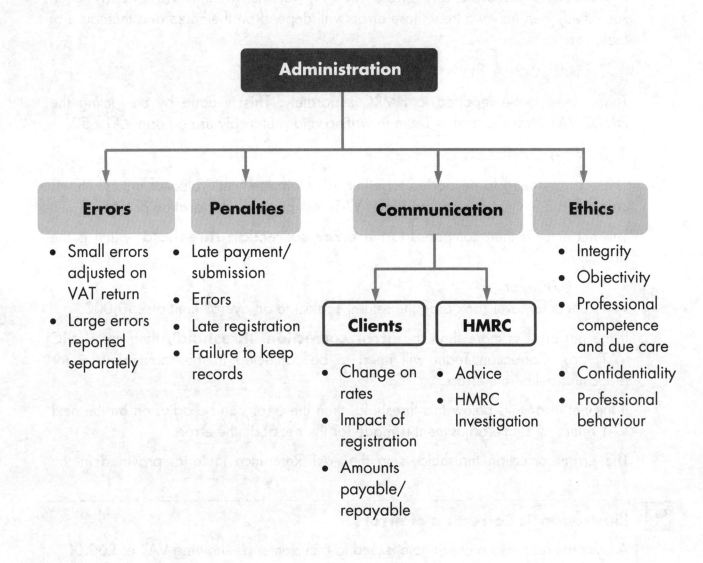

**Administration**

**Errors**
- Small errors adjusted on VAT return
- Large errors reported separately

**Penalties**
- Late payment/ submission
- Errors
- Late registration
- Failure to keep records

**Communication**

**Clients**
- Change on rates
- Impact of registration
- Amounts payable/ repayable

**HMRC**
- Advice
- HMRC Investigation

**Ethics**
- Integrity
- Objectivity
- Professional competence and due care
- Confidentiality
- Professional behaviour

# 1 Errors

If a business discovers any errors on VAT returns which have already been submitted, then how we treat these errors will depend on their size and the cause of the error.

## 1.1 Deliberate Errors

These need to be reported to HMRC separately. This is done by contacting the HMRC VAT Error Correction Team in writing and preferably using Form VAT 652.

## 1.2 Non-Deliberate Errors

These errors need to be added together to obtain the 'net' value of errors. This is calculated as any under-declaration of VAT, less any over-declaration of VAT.

The net error is then compared to the **error correction threshold** which is the greater of:

- £10,000, or
- 1% of turnover (box 6 on the return) subject to an overall limit of £50,000.

If the net error is more than the **error correction 'threshold',** then the HMRC VAT Error Correction Team will need to be contacted in the same way as for disclosing deliberate errors.

If the net error falls below this threshold, then the error can be adjusted on the next VAT return. A single adjustment is made for the net of all the errors.

The error correction threshold is in the AAT Reference material provided in the exam.

---

**Illustration 1: Correction of errors**

A business recorded a credit note issued to a customer as showing VAT of £60.00 instead of the correct amount of £6.00. In the same VAT period, the business included a sales invoice with VAT of £300 twice in the sales day book.

The net error is:

| | £ |
|---|---|
| Output tax understated by £60.00 – £6.00 | 54.00 |
| Output tax overstated by £300.00 | (300.00) |
| Net error (overstatement of output tax) | 246.00 |

Output tax in box 1 in the next VAT return should be reduced by £246.00 to correct this error.

---

# Activity 1: Jim – VAT error

You discover that a sales invoice has been entered in Jim's records twice and so the VAT has been paid twice in the quarter ended 31 March X1. The amount of VAT is £450 and you are about to prepare the VAT return for the quarter ended 30 June X1. The box 6 figure on the last VAT return was £4,000.

## Required

## What action should you take? Choose ONE answer.

A     Ignore the error as it is less than 1% of the box 6 figure for the quarter ended 31 March X1.

B     Add £450 to the box 1 figure for the VAT return for the quarter ended 30 June X1.

C     Deduct £450 from the box 1 figure for the VAT return for the quarter ended 30 June X1.

D     Obtain and complete form VAT 652 'Notification of Errors in VAT Returns'.

## Solution:

# Activity 2: X Ltd error

X Ltd has turnover of £6.5 million. The output tax on its last VAT return was understated by £52,000.

## Required

## Tick ONE statement below.

|  | ✓ |
|---|---|
| A correction can be made on the next VAT return as the error is less than 1% of turnover. |  |
| A correction cannot be made on the next return as the error exceeds £10,000. |  |
| A correction cannot be made on the next return as the error exceeds £50,000. |  |

# 2 Penalties

HMRC ensure that taxable traders follow the VAT legislation by imposing fines and penalties when the trader is at fault. You need to have an awareness only of these penalties.

| Wrong doing | Disclosure |
| --- | --- |
| Careless and deliberate errors | The penalty charged for wrongdoing will be a percentage of the potential lost revenue (ie the VAT underpaid to HMRC). <br><br> This will be charged on an error, whether it was reported separately or adjusted in the next VAT return. <br><br> A trader can minimise these penalties by making unprompted disclosures to HMRC about the errors. |
| Inaccurate VAT returns | These penalties can be reduced to zero if the trader makes an unprompted disclosure to HMRC about the inaccuracies. <br><br> If the return cannot be completed on time because some information is missing, HMRC will usually permit some of the figures to be estimated and corrected in the next return. |
| Late VAT return or payment | When this first occurs, the trader is said to be in default. <br><br> A 12-month **surcharge liability notice** period is then started. <br><br> If a late payment occurs within this period, a surcharge penalty is issued and the surcharge period is reset to 12 months. <br><br> This will be a percentage of the VAT unpaid to HMRC. |
| Failure to register for VAT | Traders need to ensure that they are completing the historic and future tests on a regular basis. <br><br> Once they have identified the need to register, they must do so within 30 days of the test date. <br><br> The penalty will be based on a percentage of the VAT due from the date registration was supposed to occur. |
| Failure to keep and retain records | All records must be kept for at least six years, unless HMRC gives written permission for a shorter period. Where records have not been retained for this period, there is a maximum penalty of £3,000 per accounting period. |

## 2.1 Assessments

The majority of penalties are based on the VAT which is due to HMRC.

If no VAT return is submitted, HMRC can raise an assessment based on what it believes is owed.

The penalty is then calculated on this amount.

The trader then has 30 days to notify HMRC if the amount owed is actually bigger. If this is not achieved, then they may be liable to another penalty.

## 2.2 Fraudulent evasion of VAT

Tax evasion is a criminal offense and this will result in fines and/or (in extreme cases) imprisonment.

**Tax evasion of VAT:**

- Misleading HMRC by suppressing information or deliberately providing false information

- Illegal

**Tax avoidance:**

- Using the legislation to minimise your tax burden
- Legal

# 3 Communications

In the exam, you will need to complete a written communication to HMRC or to a client.

This communication could be on anything you have seen in your VAT studies so far, ie contacting a client to discuss what VAT is payable to HMRC and when, or it could be in respect of the following:

## 3.1 Contact with HMRC

### Seeking advice on VAT legislation

HMRC will expect tax payers to go through the following process:

(a) Check the **HMRC website** – this can usually resolve most queries
(b) Telephone the VAT helpline – with VAT registration number and postcode
(c) Write to HMRC – preferably by email.

Any communication must always be carried out in a polite and professional manner. You should always keep a record of any communication with HMRC.

### Control visits

HMRC officers may visit a VAT-registered business to determine whether their VAT records are correct and up to date. They are entitled to do the following activities:

(a) Question the business owner, or the person responsible for keeping the VAT records

(b)   Examine business records

(c)   Check the VAT return is accurate

(d)   Watch business activity.

The officer will need to contact the business owner in writing at least seven days before the visit.

## 3.2 Maintaining up-to-date VAT knowledge

Tax advisors need to keep up to date with the VAT legislation to ensure that they keep their clients compliant and avoid penalties and surcharges.

Legislation changes can be found:

(a)   On the HMRC and government websites
(b)   In direct communications with HMRC
(c)   In technical circulars within accountancy firms
(d)   In specialist journals.

Changes in practice may be identified by:

(a)   Attending CPD (Continual Professional Development) briefings
(b)   Reading relevant journals
(c)   Meeting other professionals.

## 3.3 Changes in VAT legislation

Changes to the VAT legislation can have an impact on a number of things.

### Accounting systems

If the tax rate changes, in general or just on a specific product, then the IT systems will need to be updated for the new rates.

### Customers

If the business's customers are all VAT-registered, then the change in VAT will not impact them as they will be able to recover the input VAT they have suffered. However, if they are not VAT-registered, then an increase to the VAT rate will increase the cost of that product for the customer.

### Non-VAT-registered businesses

If the VAT registration threshold changes, then this could mean that some businesses may need to register earlier or later than expected.

## Activity 3: Ian Morris – Client communication

You are a trainee accounting technician working for a sole trader, Mr Shelton. Mr Shelton has just received a letter from a client, Ian Morris (a trader making only standard-rated supplies to non-registered clients), asking about the impact of a recent change in the standard rate of VAT on his clients. The rate changed from 20% to 25%. He is undecided about whether to change his prices.

**Required**

**You are required to complete the following letter to Ian Morris discussing the options open to him.**

To:        Ian Morris
From:      Mr Shelton
Date:      30 December
Subject:   Change of VAT rate

Dear Ian Morris,

Further to your recent email, I have set out below the options open to you in relation to the standard rate of VAT.

Until recently, you have been charging VAT at a rate of [ _____ ] . Therefore a VAT-exclusive sale with a value of £1,000 has cost your non-registered clients £ [ _____ ] .

The two options open to you are as follows:

- Keep the same VAT-exclusive value of £1,000.

  The benefit of this option is that you have the same amount of VAT-exclusive sales value per item sold. However, this will now make the VAT-inclusive cost to your customers higher at £ [ _____ ] . This may make your prices less competitive (if your competitors do not do the same) and may result in a loss of some customers.

- Keep the same VAT-inclusive value of £ [ _____ ] .

  Under this alternative option, you will remain competitive to your customers. However, your VAT-exclusive sales value per item sold will be reduced to £ [ _____ ] .

There is no obvious correct option to choose; it will depend primarily on the strength of your competitors.

If you wish to discuss this with me in more detail, please do not hesitate to contact me.

Yours sincerely,

Mr Shelton

**Picklists:**

| (1) | 0% | 20% | 25% |
|-----|------|------|------|
| (2) | 1,000 | 1,200 | 1,500 |
| (3) | 1,000 | 1,200 | 1,250 |
| (4) | 1,000 | 1,200 | 1,250 |
| (5) | 1,000 | 960 | 800 |

# 4 Ethics

## 4.1 Fundamental principles

Working in tax requires adherence to the following five fundamental ethical principles:

- **Integrity:** being straightforward and honest in all business relationships

- **Objectivity:** refusing to allow bias, conflicts of interest or undue influence to override professional judgements

- **Professional competence and due care:** a professional accountant has an obligation to keep their knowledge and skills at a level that enables clients to receive a competent professional service, and to act diligently when providing those services

- **Confidentiality:** respecting the confidentiality of client information, and keeping it confidential unless there is a legal or professional obligation to disclose it

- **Professional behaviour:** compliance with relevant laws and regulations to avoid discrediting the profession.

## Activity 4: Fundamental principles

You work in the tax department of a large company. You have prepared the VAT return for the quarter, and submitted it to your finance director for her review. On reviewing your draft return, she has asked you to amend it in order reclaim all the VAT on a party, at which several clients were in attendance. She mentioned at the end of the conversation that your annual performance appraisal was due.

**Required**

**Which fundamental principle(s) could be breached if you agreed to her request?**

**Tick THREE Boxes.**

| | ✓ |
|---|---|
| Integrity | |
| Objectivity | |
| Professional competence and due care | |
| Confidentiality | |
| Professional behaviour | |

## Chapter summary

- If a net error smaller than the error correction reporting threshold is discovered from a previous tax period, it can be corrected in the next VAT return.

- If a net error exceeding the error correction reporting threshold is discovered from a previous tax period, it cannot be adjusted in the next VAT return. Instead, a voluntary disclosure should be made and the HMRC VAT Error Correction Team informed. A penalty might be imposed, depending on the behaviour of the business.

- If a VAT return or payment is late, the taxpayer is served with a surcharge liability notice which lasts for 12 months. If further payment defaults occur within that 12 months, there may be a surcharge to pay, and the notice is extended to 12 months again.

- A number of other penalties pertain to VAT, including failure to register and failure to keep records.

- VAT evasion is a criminal offence and may give rise to fines and/or imprisonment.

- VAT can be a substantial payment for a business. Therefore steps must be taken to ensure both the return and payment can be made by the due dates.

- Changes in VAT legislation can have a significant impact on accounting systems.

- Staff and customers need to be informed of a change to the VAT rate.

- HMRC expect taxpayers to try and resolve any queries by checking their website before telephoning or writing to them. However, sometimes written confirmation about an issue should be insisted upon.

- HMRC officers may, from time to time, visit a VAT-registered business to check on VAT records.

- It is important to maintain up-to-date knowledge of changes to VAT legislation and practice.

## Keywords

- **Error correction threshold:** this is the threshold that dictates whether errors discovered on a previous return can be corrected on the next return or must be reported separately

- **Evasion of VAT:** falsely reclaiming input VAT/understating output tax, obtaining bad debt relief or obtaining a repayment

- **HMRC website:** the first place a taxpayer must check to try and resolve any VAT queries

- **Surcharge liability notice:** this warns a business that its VAT return or payment was not received on time and if the business pays late within the next 12 months, a default surcharge will be due

## Activity answers

### Activity 1: Jim – VAT error

C    Deduct £450 from the box 1 figure for the VAT return for the quarter ended 30 June X1. A is wrong as an error should never be ignored; the 1% threshold applies to whether the error can be rectified on the return or should be notified separately, not to whether the error should be corrected at all. B would duplicate the error and D is not required as the error is less than £10,000 which itself is greater than 1% of the box 6 figure (ie £40).

### Activity 2: X Ltd Error

|  | ✓ |
|---|---|
| A correction can be made on the next VAT return as the error is less than 1% of turnover. | |
| A correction cannot be made on the next return as the error exceeds £10,000. | |
| A correction cannot be made on the next return as the error exceeds £50,000. | ✓ |

The error is less than 1% of turnover, but that is subject to an overall limit of £50,000.

### Activity 3: Ian Morris – Client communications

To:        Ian Morris
From:    Mr Shelton
Date:     30 December
Subject:  Change of VAT rate

Dear Ian Morris,

Further to your recent email, I have set out below the options open to you in relation to the standard-rate of VAT.

Until recently, you have been charging VAT at a rate of $\boxed{20\%}$. Therefore, a VAT-exclusive sale with a value of £1,000 has cost your non-registered clients $\boxed{£1,200}$.

The two options open to you are as follows:

*   Keep the same VAT-exclusive value of £1,000.

    The benefit of this option is that you have the same amount of VAT-exclusive sales value per item sold. However, this will now make the VAT-inclusive cost to your customers higher at $\boxed{£1,250}$. This may make your prices less competitive (if your competitors do not do the same) and may result in a loss of some customers.

- Keep the same VAT-inclusive value of $\boxed{\textbf{£1,200}}$.

    Under this alternative option, you will remain competitive to your customers. However, your VAT-exclusive sales value per item sold will be reduced to $\boxed{\textbf{£960}}$ **(Working)**.

There is no obvious correct option to choose, it will depend primarily on the strength of your competitors.

If you wish to discuss this with me in more detail, please do not hesitate to contact me.

Yours sincerely,

Mr Shelton

**Working**

£1,200 × 100/125 = £960

## Activity 4: Fundamental Principles

| | ✓ |
|---|---|
| Integrity | ✓ |
| Objectivity | ✓ |
| Professional competence and due care | |
| Confidentiality | |
| Professional behaviour | ✓ |

Integrity: It would not be honest to knowingly reclaim an excessive amount of input tax

Objectivity: Agreeing to the finance director's request because of the impact on job prospects, would be to allow bias to affect judgement

Professional behaviour: Submitting a tax return that does not follow tax law is illegal

## Test your learning

1 **Identify which one of the following statements is correct.**

| | ✓ |
|---|---|
| If a net error of more than the lower of £10,000 and 1% of turnover (subject to an overall £5,000 limit) is discovered, it must be disclosed on Form VAT 652. | |
| If a net error of more than the greater of £10,000 and 1% of turnover (subject to an overall £5,000 limit) is discovered, it must be disclosed on Form VAT 652. | |
| If a net error of more than the lower of £10,000 and 1% of turnover (subject to an overall £50,000 limit) is discovered, it must be disclosed on Form VAT 652. | |
| If a net error of more than the greater of £10,000 and 1% of turnover (subject to an overall £50,000 limit) is discovered it must be disclosed on Form VAT 652. | |

2 **Identify whether the following statement is true or false.**

Tax avoidance is illegal and could lead to fines and/or imprisonment.

| True ✓ | False ✓ |
|---|---|
| | |

3 You are a trainee accounting technician working for a sole trader, Mr Smith.
Mr Smith has just received a letter from a client, Michael James (a trader making only standard-rated supplies to non-VAT-registered clients) asking about the impact of a recent change in the standard rate of VAT on his clients. The rate changed from 20% to 18%. He is undecided about whether to change his prices.

**You are required to complete the following letter to Michael James, discussing the options open to him.**

Mr Smith<br>
Number Street<br>
London<br>
SW11 8AB

Mr James
Alphabet Street
London
W12 6WM

Dear Mr James

CHANGE IN THE STANDARD RATE OF VAT

Further to your recent letter, I have set out below the options open to you in relation to the standard rate of VAT.

Until recently, you have been charging VAT at a rate of [            ] (1) Therefore a VAT-exclusive sale with a value of £1,000 has cost your non-VAT-registered clients £ [            ] (2) (£1,000 plus VAT).

The two options open to you are as follows:

- Keep the same VAT-exclusive value of £1,000.

  Under this option, you would have the same amount of VAT-exclusive sales value per item sold. However, this will now make the VAT-inclusive cost to your customers lower at [            ] (3). You have effectively passed on the VAT saving to your customers.

- Keep the same VAT-inclusive value of £ [            ] (4).

  Under this alternative option, you are not passing the VAT saving to your customers, which they may query, especially if your competitors reduce their prices. However, the benefit of this option is that your VAT-exclusive sales value per item sold will be increased to [            ] (5).

There is no obvious correct option to choose; it will depend primarily on the actions of your competitors.

If you wish to discuss this with me in more detail, please do not hesitate to contact me.

Yours sincerely

Mr Smith

**Picklists:**

(1)  10% / 20% / 25%

(2)  1,000 / 1,200 / 1,250

(3)  £1,000 / £1,200 (£1,000 plus VAT at 20%) / £1,180 (£1,000 plus VAT at 18%)

(4)  1,000 / 1,200 / 1,180

(5)  £1,000 (£1,200 × 100/120) / £1,016.95 (£1,200 × 100/118)

4  A taxpayer should try and resolve a VAT query in the following order:

**Fill in the blank space from the picklist below.**

| | | |
|---|---|---|
| Firstly... | | ▼ |
| If no luck, then... | | ▼ |
| Still cannot resolve, then... | | ▼ |

**Picklist:**

Check HMRC website
Ring the HMRC VAT helpline
Write to or email HMRC

5  **Identify which one of the following statements is correct.**

| | ✓ |
|---|---|
| A VAT officer will usually turn up for a control visit unannounced. | |
| A VAT officer can check the correct amount of VAT has been paid or reclaimed. | |
| A VAT officer is not entitled to examine the business records. | |

6  A business made a 'small' overstatement of input tax on a previous return.

**What effect will this have on the current VAT payable to HMRC?**

| | ✓ |
|---|---|
| An increase in the VAT payable via the current return. | |
| A decrease in the VAT payable via the current return. | |
| No impact on the current return. It must simply be separately declared. | |

7  A business made a 'small' understatement of output tax on a previous return.

**Should this adjustment be shown on the latest VAT return, and if so, where on the return?**

| | ✓ |
|---|---|
| No – not shown on the return | |
| Yes – shown in box 1 | |
| Yes – shown in box 4 | |

## 8 VAT account

| Date 20XX | Reference | Debit £ | Date 20XX | Reference | Credit £ |
|---|---|---|---|---|---|
| 1.1-31.3 | Sales returns day book | 474.80 | 1.1-31.3 | Sales day book | 10,422.20 |
| 1.1-31.3 | Purchases day book | 3,596.00 | 1.1-31.3 | Cash book – UK sales | 2,069.00 |
| 31.3 | Bad debt relief | 195.00 | 1.1-31.3 | Purchases returns day book – UK purchases | 204.00 |
| 31.3 | EU acquisition reclaim | 651.20 | 31.3 | Fuel scale charge | 28.83 |
| 31.3 | BALANCE b/d | 8,458.23 | 31.3 | EU acquisition charge | 651.20 |
| | **Total** | **13,375.23** | | **Total** | **13,375.23** |
| | | | | VAT payable | 8,458.23 |

**Following on from the example in Chapter 5, use the above VAT account to complete the email below.**

To:        Finance Director
From:      Accounting Technician
Date:      25 April 20XX
Subject    VAT return to 31 March 20XX

Please be advised that I have now completed the VAT return for the quarter to 31 March 20XX. If you are in agreement with the figures shown in the return, please could you arrange an electronic payment of £ [          ] to be made by [          ] (1)

If you wish to discuss this further, please feel free to call me.

Kind regards

**Picklist:**

(1)   30 April 20XX / 7 May 20XX / 7 June 20XX

9 Doug is a retailer and has been selling goods to the general public for £235 (VAT-inclusive) while the VAT rate was 17.5%. (VAT fraction 7/47). When the VAT rate changed to 20% he did not want to change the cost of these goods to his customers who are not VAT-registered.

**Work out for Doug the VAT-exclusive amount of the goods sold both before and after the change in the VAT rate.**

| VAT-inclusive £ | VAT rate | VAT-exclusive £ |
|---|---|---|
| 235.00 | 17.5% | |
| 235.00 | 20% | |

## Test your learning: answers

# Chapter 1    Introduction to VAT

1

|  | ✓ |
| --- | --- |
| HM Customs & Excise | |
| Inland Revenue | |
| HM Revenue & Customs | ✓ |
| HM Treasury | |

2

|  | ✓ |
| --- | --- |
| Output VAT is the VAT charged by a supplier on the sales that are made by his business. Output VAT is collected by the supplier and paid over to HMRC. | ✓ |
| Output VAT is the VAT suffered by the purchaser of the goods which will be reclaimed from HMRC if the purchaser is VAT-registered. | |

The other statement describes input VAT.

3    VAT is collected by HMRC throughout the manufacturing/supply chain for goods. Each VAT-registered business that buys, processes and then sells the goods pays the difference between the VAT on their sale and the VAT on their purchase over to HMRC.

# Chapter 2    VAT Basics

1

|  | True ✓ | False ✓ |
| --- | --- | --- |
| If a business supplies zero-rated services then the business is not able to reclaim the VAT on its purchases and expenses from HMRC. | | ✓ |
| A business makes zero-rated supplies. The cost to the business of its purchases and expenses is the VAT-exclusive amount. | ✓ | |

2

| | | Register without delay | Register within 30 days | Monitor and register later |
|---|---|---|---|---|
| A | An existing business with total turnover for the previous 11 months of £80,000. Sales for the next month are unknown at present. | | | ✓ |
| B | A new business with an expected turnover for the next 30 days of £90,000 | ✓ | | |
| C | An existing business with total turnover for the previous 12 months of £7,250 per month | | ✓ | |

3

AN Accountant
Number Street
London
SW11 8AB

Mrs Quirke
Alphabet Street
London
W12 6WM

Dear Mrs Quirke

VAT REGISTRATION

Further to our recent telephone conversation, set out below are the circumstances when you must register your business for VAT.

If the taxable turnover of your business at the end of a month, looking back no more than **twelve** months, has exceeded the registration limit of **£83,000**, then the business must apply to register for VAT within 30 days.

Alternatively, if at any time, the taxable turnover (before any VAT is added) is expected to exceed the registration limit within the next **30 days** alone, then the business must apply to be registered for VAT without delay. This would be the situation if, for example, you obtained a large additional contract for, say, £85,000.

If you wish to discuss this in any more detail, please do not hesitate to contact me.

Yours sincerely

AN Accountant

4    **By what date will Amy exceed the threshold for VAT?**

| 30 April 2017 |
|---|

**By what date must Amy register for VAT?**

| 30 May 2017 |
|---|

VAT registration is required when taxable supplies (standard plus zero-rated supplies) exceed £83,000. Taxable supplies are £9,320 (£7,850 + £1,470) per month.

Amy exceeds this threshold after 9 months, ie by 30 April 2017 as taxable supplies are then £83,880 (9 × £9,320).

5

| | ✓ |
|---|---|
| At the beginning of month 12, Richard expects his taxable supplies to exceed £83,000 in the next 30 days. | |
| At the end of month 12, Richard's taxable supplies in the previous 12 months will have exceeded £83,000. | ✓ |

The historic test is met at the end of month 12.

For the future test to be met, the taxable supplies in the next 30 days alone must exceed the threshold, ie the taxable supplies in the previous 11 months are not included. Therefore, the future test is not met here.

6

| | ✓ |
|---|---|
| Preparation of VAT returns would be optional. | |
| Customers would benefit by being able to claim back input VAT. | |
| Business would benefit by being able to claim back input VAT. | ✓ |

Once registered, even voluntarily, VAT returns will have to be completed.

VAT-registered customers would neither gain nor lose because they could reclaim VAT charged to them, and non-VAT-registered customers would be disadvantaged because they would be charged VAT they could not reclaim.

# Chapter 3   Inputs and outputs

1

(a)

| The VAT is £76.80 |
|---|

VAT    =    £384.00 × 20%
       =    £76.80

(b)

| | Output tax ✓ | Input tax ✓ |
|---|---|---|
| Business C | ✓ | |
| Business D | | ✓ |

2

| | ✓ |
|---|---|
| Staff party | |
| Car for sales manager | ✓ |
| Photocopier | |
| Entertaining UK clients | ✓ |

3

| VAT-inclusive £ | VAT at 20 % £ |
|---|---|
| 42.88 | 7.14 |
| 96.57 | 16.09 |
| 28.20 | 4.70 |
| 81.07 | 13.51 |

(a)  £42.88 × 1/6  =  £7.14
(b)  £96.57 × 1/6  =  £16.09
(c)  £28.20 × 1/6  =  £4.70
(d)  £81.07 × 1/6  =  £13.51

4

| | ✓ |
|---|---|
| The goods will be treated as standard-rated in the UK if the American business is VAT-registered. | |
| The goods will be treated as standard-rated in the UK, provided documentary evidence of the export is obtained within three months. | |
| The goods will be treated as zero-rated in the UK if the American business is VAT-registered. | |
| The goods will be treated as zero-rated in the UK, provided documentary evidence of the export is obtained within three months. | ✓ |

5

| Net £ | VAT rate % | VAT £ | Gross £ |
|---|---|---|---|
| 43.50 | 20 | 8.70 | 52.20 |
| 18.00 | 20 | 3.60 | 21.60 |

**Workings**

VAT  =  £52.20 × 1/6          VAT  =  £18.00 × 20%

=  £8.70                    =  £3.60

6

| | True ✓ | False ✓ |
|---|---|---|
| A VAT-registered business can reclaim all the input VAT attributed to zero-rated supplies. | ✓ | |
| A VAT-registered business can reclaim all the input VAT attributed to standard-rated supplies. | ✓ | |
| A VAT-registered business can reclaim all the input VAT attributed to exempt supplies. | | ✓ |
| A VAT-registered business can reclaim all the input VAT attributed to both taxable and exempt supplies providing, certain *de minimis* tests are satisfied. | ✓ | |

7

| | ✓ |
|---|---|
| No VAT is charged by the EU supplier; therefore this can be ignored by Joe on his VAT return. | |
| Joe must pay output VAT to HMRC at the port/airport and can reclaim input VAT on the next return. | |
| Joe must charge himself 'output VAT' and 'reclaim input' VAT on the same return. | ✓ |

# Chapter 4 Accounting for VAT

1

|  | ✓ |
| --- | --- |
| 1 year | |
| 2 years | |
| 6 years | ✓ |
| 20 years | |

2

|  | ✓ |
| --- | --- |
| A proforma invoice is always sent out when goods are sent to customers, before issuing the proper invoice. | |
| A proforma invoice should always include the words 'This is not a VAT invoice'. | ✓ |
| A customer can reclaim VAT stated on a proforma invoice. | |
| A proforma invoice is sent out to offer a customer the chance to purchase the goods detailed. | ✓ |

3

|  | Date | Basic (B)/ Actual (A) |
| --- | --- | --- |
| An invoice is sent out to a customer for goods on 22 June 20X0 and the goods are despatched on 29 June 20X0. | 22 June | A |
| Goods are sent out to a customer on 18 June 20X0 and this is followed by an invoice on 23 June 20X0. | 23 June | A |
| A customer pays in full for goods on 27 June 20X0 and they are then delivered to the customer on 2 July 20X0. | 27 June | A |

4

|  | ✓ |
| --- | --- |
| 15 May 20X0 | |
| 20 May 20X0 | ✓ |
| 20 June 20X0 | |

The earliest date is despatch on 15 May. As the invoice is sent within 14 days, the invoice date becomes the tax point.

5

|  | ✓ |
|---|---|
| 2 June 20X0 | ✓ |
| 11 June 20X0 | ✓ |
| 29 June 20X0 | |
| 31 July 20X0 | |

### Deposit

The cash paid for the deposit is the earliest date so 2 June is the tax point for the deposit.

### Balance

Despatch is the earliest date relating to the balancing payment. This is not over-ridden by the invoice date as the invoice is sent more than 14 days later. So the despatch date of 11 June is the tax point for the balancing payment.

6

The VAT on a bad debt can be reclaimed from HMRC when the following conditions are met:

- The debt is more than six months overdue and less than four years and six months old

- The original VAT on the invoice has been paid to HMRC

- The debt is written-off in the accounts of the business.

# Chapter 5   The VAT return

1

|  | True ✓ | False ✓ |
|---|---|---|
| If input VAT is greater than output VAT on the return, VAT is payable to HMRC. | | ✓ |
| If output VAT is greater than input VAT on the return, VAT is repayable from HMRC. | | ✓ |

If input VAT is greater than output VAT on the return then VAT is repayable, and if output VAT is greater than input VAT on the return, then VAT is payable to HMRC.

**2**

| | ✓ |
|---|---|
| The payment of £4,700 for the previous quarter has been included twice in the VAT account | |
| The payment of £4,700 for the previous quarter has been omitted from the VAT account | ✓ |

By omitting the VAT paid debit of £4,700.00, the balance on the account is showing as £12,220.00 instead of the correct £7,520.00.

| Date 20XX | Reference | Debit £ | Date 20XX | Reference | Credit £ |
|---|---|---|---|---|---|
| QTR 1 | VAT paid | | QTR 1 | VAT payable | 4,700.00 |
| | | | QTR 2 | VAT payable | 7,520.00 |
| | Balance | 12,220.00 | | | |
| | **Total** | **12,220.00** | | **Total** | **12,220.00** |
| | | | QTR 2 | VAT payable | 12,220.00 |

**3**

| VAT return for quarter ended 30.6.20XX | | £ |
|---|---|---|
| VAT due in this period on **sales** and other outputs | Box 1 | 7,520.00 |
| VAT due in this period on **acquisitions** from other **EC Member States** | Box 2 | 750.00 |
| Total VAT due (**the sum of boxes 1 and 2**) | Box 3 | 8,270.00 |
| VAT reclaimed in this period on **purchases** and other inputs, including acquisitions from the EC | Box 4 | 3,950.00 |
| Net VAT to be paid to HM Revenue & Customs or reclaimed by you (**Difference between boxes 3 and 4 – if box 4 is greater than box 3, use a minus sign**) | Box 5 | 4,320.00 |
| Total value of **sales** and all other outputs, excluding any VAT. **Include your box 8 figure. Whole pounds only** | Box 6 | 43,400 |

| VAT return for quarter ended 30.6.20XX | | £ |
|---|---|---|
| Total value of **purchases** and all other inputs, excluding any VAT. **Include your box 9 figure. Whole pounds only** | Box 7 | 19,250 |
| Total value of all **supplies** of goods and related costs, excluding any VAT, to other **EC Member States. Whole pounds only** | Box 8 | 0 |
| Total value of all **acquisitions** of goods and related costs, excluding any VAT, from other **EC Member States. Whole pounds only** | Box 9 | 3,750 |

## Workings

| | | £ |
|---|---|---|
| Box 1 | VAT on sales from the sales day book | 5,200.00 |
| | VAT on sales from the cash book | 2,800.00 |
| | Less: VAT on credit notes | (480.00) |
| | | 7,520.00 |
| Box 2 | VAT due on EU acquisitions | 750.00 |
| Box 3 | Total of box 1 and box 2 £7,520.00 + £750.00 | 8,270.00 |
| Box 4 | VAT on purchases from purchases day book | 3,100.00 |
| | VAT on EU acquisitions | 750.00 |
| | Bad debt relief (£500.00 × 20%) | 100.00 |
| | | 3,950.00 |
| Box 5 | Net VAT due box 3 minus box 4 | |
| | £8,270.00 – £3,950.00 | 4,320.00 |
| Box 6 | Standard-rated credit UK sales | 26,000.00 |
| | Less: Standard-rated credit notes | (2,400.00) |
| | Cash sales | 14,000.00 |
| | Exports | 5,800.00 |
| | | 43,400 |

|  | | £ |
|---|---|---:|
| Box 7 | Standard-rated credit purchases | 15,500.00 |
|  | EU acquisitions | 3,750.00 |
|  |  | 19,250 |
| Box 8 | EU sales | 0 |
| Box 9 | EU acquisitions | 3,750 |

4

| VAT return for quarter ended 31.5.20XX |  | £ |
|---|---|---:|
| VAT due in this period on **sales** and other outputs | Box 1 | 7,066.78 |
| VAT due in this period on **acquisitions** from other **EC Member States** | Box 2 | 0 |
| Total VAT due **(the sum of boxes 1 and 2)** | Box 3 | 7,066.78 |
| VAT reclaimed in this period on **purchases** and other inputs, including acquisitions from the EC | Box 4 | 4,735.17 |
| Net VAT to be paid to HM Revenue & Customs or reclaimed by you **(Difference between boxes 3 and 4 – if box 4 is greater than box 3, use a minus sign)** | Box 5 | 2,331.61 |
| Total value of **sales** and all other outputs excluding any VAT. **Include your box 8 figure. Whole pounds only** | Box 6 | 38,890 |
| Total value of **purchases** and all other inputs excluding any VAT. **Include your box 9 figure. Whole pounds only** | Box 7 | 26,154 |
| Total value of all **supplies** of goods and related costs, excluding any VAT, to other **EC Member States. Whole pounds only** | Box 8 | 0 |
| Total value of all **acquisitions** of goods and related costs, excluding any VAT, from other **EC Member States. Whole pounds only** | Box 9 | 0 |

**Tutorial note:** In past assessments, the entries for boxes 6–9 have been accepted, whether rounded up or down to the nearest pound. However, if the task does give particular instructions on rounding, then these instructions should be followed.

## Workings

|  |  | £ |
|---|---|---|
| **Box 1** | VAT on sales from the sales day book | 6,135.65 |
|  | VAT on sales from the cash book | 1,010.90 |
|  | Less: VAT on credit notes | (79.77) |
|  |  | 7,066.78 |
| **Box 2** | VAT due on EU acquisitions | 0 |
| **Box 3** | Total of box 1 and box 2 | 7,066.78 |
| **Box 4** | VAT on purchases from purchases day book | 4,090.17 |
|  | VAT on purchases from cash payments book | 606.60 |
|  | Bad debt relief | 38.40 |
|  |  | 4,735.17 |
| **Box 5** | Net VAT due box 3 minus box 4 | 2,331.61 |
| **Box 6** | Zero-rated credit UK sales | 3,581.67 |
|  | Standard-rated credit UK sales | 30,678.25 |
|  | Cash sales | 5,054.51 |
|  | Less: Zero-rated credit notes | (25.59) |
|  | Less: Standard-rated credit notes | (398.86) |
|  |  | 38,890 |
| **Box 7** | Zero-rated credit UK purchases | 2,669.80 |
|  | Standard-rated credit UK purchases | 20,450.85 |
|  | Cash purchases | 3,033.01 |
|  |  | 26,154 |
| **Box 8** | EU sales | 0 |
| **Box 9** | EU acquisitions | 0 |

BPP
LEARNING MEDIA

5

| | ✓ |
|---|---|
| Input tax paid at the ports is reclaimed as input tax on the VAT return. | |
| Both input tax and output tax in relation to the goods are shown on the VAT return. | ✓ |
| They are zero-rated and so no VAT features on the VAT return. | |
| They are exempt and so no VAT features on the VAT return. | |

6

| | ✓ |
|---|---|
| The fuel scale charge increases output VAT and is shown in box 1. | ✓ |
| VAT on EU acquisitions increases both input VAT and output VAT and is shown in boxes 1 and 4. | |
| Credit notes received from suppliers reduce input VAT and are shown in box 4. | ✓ |
| Credit notes issued to customers reduce output VAT and are shown in box 1. | ✓ |

VAT on EU acquisitions increases both input VAT and output VAT, but is shown in boxes 2 and 4.

7

| VAT return for quarter ended 31.03.20X0 | | £ |
|---|---|---|
| VAT due in this period on sales and other outputs. | Box 1 | 6,880.00 |
| Total value of sales and all other outputs, excluding any VAT. Include your box 8 figure. Whole pounds only. | Box 6 | 62,450 |
| Total value of all supplies of goods and related costs, excluding any VAT, to other EC Member States. Whole pounds only. | Box 8 | 18,345 |

Box 1 = (27,200 + 7,200) × 20%

Box 6 = 27,200 + 9,705 + 18,345 + 7,200

Box 8 = 18,345

8

| VAT return for quarter ended 31/3/X0 | | £ |
|---|---|---|
| VAT due in this period on acquisitions from other EC Member States | Box 2 | 1,669.00 |
| VAT reclaimed in this period on purchases and other inputs, including acquisitions from the EC | Box 4 | 3,756.00 |
| Total value of purchases and all other inputs excluding any VAT. Include your box 9 figure. Whole pounds only | Box 7 | 18,780 |
| Total value of all acquisitions of goods and related costs, excluding any VAT, from other EC Member States. Whole pounds only | Box 9 | 8,345 |

Box 2 = 8,345 × 20%

Box 4 = (9,230 + 1,205 + 8,345) × 20%

Box 7 = 9,230 + 1,205 + 8,345

Box 9 = 8,345

# CHAPTER 6   Schemes for small businesses

1

AN accountant
Number Street
London
SW11 8AB

Mr Lymstock
Alphabet Street
London
W12 6WM

Dear Mr Lymstock

ANNUAL ACCOUNTING SCHEME

I have recently been reviewing your files. I would like to make you aware of a scheme that you could use for VAT.

As the annual value of your taxable supplies, **excluding** VAT and supplies of capital items, in the following 12 months is expected to be **no more than £1,350,000** you can join the annual accounting scheme.

Under this scheme, you make **nine** monthly direct debit payments based on your VAT liability for the previous year. The first of these payments is due at the end of the | **fourth** | month of the accounting period. You must then prepare a VAT return for the year and submit it in with the balancing payment, by | **two months** | after the year end.

Use of this annual accounting scheme is a great help, as it means that you only have to prepare | **one** | VAT return(s) each year.

If you wish to discuss this with me in more detail, please do not hesitate to contact me.

Yours sincerely

AN Accountant

2

If the annual value of taxable supplies, | **excluding** | VAT, is | **no more** | than | **£1,350,000** | and provided that a trader has a clean record with HMRC, he may be able to apply to use the cash accounting scheme.

The scheme allows the accounting for VAT to be based upon the date of | **receipt and payment of money** |. This is particularly useful for a business which gives its customers a | **long** | period of credit whilst paying its suppliers promptly.

The scheme also gives automatic relief | **for bad debts** | so if the customer does not pay the amount due, then the VAT need not be accounted for to HMRC.

3

(a)

|  | ✓ |
|---|---|
| £897.00 |  |
| £1,092.50 |  |
| £1,311.00 | ✓ |

**Working**

£9,500 × 120 % × 11.5% = £1,311.00

(b)

|  | ✓ |
|---|---|
| More VAT is payable not using the flat rate scheme |  |
| More VAT is payable using the flat rate scheme | ✓ |

## Working

If not using the flat rate scheme, the VAT payable would be:

|  |  | £ |
|---|---|---|
| Output tax | £9,500 × 20% | 1,900.00 |
| Input tax | £3,000 × 20% | (600.00) |
|  |  | 1,300.00 |

4

|  | True ✓ | False ✓ |
|---|---|---|
| The first payment due to HMRC is by 1 April 2015. |  | ✓ |

The first payment due to HMRC is by 30 April 2015 (ie the **end** of month 4).

5

|  | ✓ |
|---|---|
| Yes, because they would be able to reclaim input VAT earlier |  |
| Yes, because they would pay output VAT later |  |
| No, because they would reclaim input VAT later | ✓ |
| No, because they would pay output VAT earlier |  |

5

|  | ✓ |
|---|---|
| £2,550 |  |
| £3,060 | ✓ |

The VAT due to HMRC is 8.5% of the VAT-inclusive figure.

(£30,000 × 120%) × 8.5% = £3,060

# CHAPTER 7   Administration

**1**

The correct statement is:

| | ✓ |
|---|---|
| If a net error of more than the lower of £10,000 and 1% of turnover (subject to an overall £5,000 limit) is discovered, it must be disclosed on Form VAT 652. | |
| If a net error of more than the greater of £10,000 and 1% of turnover (subject to an overall £5,000 limit) is discovered, it must be disclosed on Form VAT 652. | |
| If a net error of more than the lower of £10,000 and 1% of turnover (subject to an overall £50,000 limit) is discovered, it must be disclosed on Form VAT 652. | |
| If a net error of more than the greater of £10,000 and 1% of turnover (subject to an overall £50,000 limit) is discovered, it must be disclosed on Form VAT 652. | ✓ |

**2**

| True ✓ | False ✓ |
|---|---|
| | ✓ |

Tax **evasion** is illegal and could lead to fines and/or imprisonment, as opposed to tax **avoidance.**

**3**

Mr Smith
Number Street
London
SW11 8AB

Mr James
Alphabet Street
London
W12 6WM

Dear Mr James

CHANGE IN THE STANDARD RATE OF VAT

Further to your recent letter, I have set out below the options open to you in relation to the standard rate of VAT.

Until recently, you have been charging VAT at a rate of [ **20%** ]. Therefore a VAT-exclusive sale with a value of £1,000 has cost your non-VAT-registered clients [ **£1,200** ] (£1,000 plus VAT).

The two options open to you are as follows:

- Keep the same VAT-exclusive value of [ **£1,000** ].

  Under this option, you would have the same amount of VAT-exclusive sales value per item sold. However, this will now make the VAT-inclusive cost to your customers lower at [ **£1,180** ] (£1,000 plus VAT at 18%). You have effectively passed on the VAT saving to your customers.

- Under this alternative option, you are not passing the VAT saving to your customers, which they may query, especially if your competitors reduce their prices. However, the benefit of this option is that your VAT-exclusive sales value per item sold will be increased to [ **£1,016.95** ] £1,016.95 (£1,200 × 100/118).

There is no obvious correct option to choose; it will depend primarily on the actions of your competitors.

If you wish to discuss this with me in more detail, please do not hesitate to contact me.

Yours sincerely

Mr Smith

4

A taxpayer should try and resolve a VAT query in the following order:

| Firstly... | Check HMRC website |
|---|---|
| If no luck, then... | Ring the HMRC VAT helpline |
| Still cannot resolve, then... | Write to or email HMRC |

5

| | ✓ |
|---|---|
| A VAT officer will usually turn up for a control visit unannounced. | |
| A VAT officer can check the correct amount of VAT has been paid or reclaimed. | ✓ |
| A VAT officer is not entitled to examine the business records. | |

**6**

| | ✓ |
|---|---|
| An increase in the VAT payable via the current return. | ✓ |
| A decrease in the VAT payable via the current return. | |
| No impact on the current return. It must simply be separately declared. | |

**7**

| | ✓ |
|---|---|
| No – not shown on the return | |
| Yes – shown in box 1 | ✓ |
| Yes – shown in box 4 | |

It is shown as an increase in the output tax at box 1 on the VAT return.

**8**

To: Finance Director
From: Accounting Technician
Date: 25 April 20XX
Subject VAT return to 31 March 20XX

Please be advised that I have now completed the VAT return for the quarter to 31 March 20XX. If you are in agreement with the figures shown in the return, please could you arrange an electronic payment of £8,458.23 to be made by 7 May 20XX.

If you wish to discuss this further, please feel free to call me.
Kind regards

**9**

| VAT-inclusive £ | VAT rate | VAT-exclusive £ |
|---|---|---|
| 235.00 | 17.5% | 200.00 |
| 235.00 | 20% | 195.83 |

**Workings**

- VAT rate of 17.5% (VAT fraction 7/47 or 17.5/117.5)

  VAT-exclusive value £235 – (7/47 × £235) = £200

- VAT rate of 20% (VAT fraction 1/6 or 20/120)

  VAT-exclusive value £235 – (1/6 × £235) = £195.83

# Index

## REVIEW FORM

**How have you used this Course Book?**
*(Tick one box only)*

☐ Self study

☐ On a course_____

☐ Other _____

**Why did you decide to purchase this Course Book?** *(Tick one box only)*

☐ Have used BPP materials in the past

☐ Recommendation by friend/colleague

☐ Recommendation by a college lecturer

☐ Saw advertising

☐ Other _____

**During the past six months do you recall seeing/receiving either of the following?**
*(Tick as many boxes as are relevant)*

☐ Our advertisement in Accounting Technician

☐ Our Publishing Catalogue

**Which (if any) aspects of our advertising do you think are useful?**
*(Tick as many boxes as are relevant)*

☐ Prices and publication dates of new editions

☐ Information on Course Book content

☐ Details of our free online offering

☐ None of the above

**Your ratings, comments and suggestions would be appreciated on the following areas of this Course Book.**

|  | Very useful | Useful | Not useful |
|---|---|---|---|
| Chapter overviews | ☐ | ☐ | ☐ |
| Introductory section | ☐ | ☐ | ☐ |
| Quality of explanations | ☐ | ☐ | ☐ |
| Illustrations | ☐ | ☐ | ☐ |
| Chapter activities | ☐ | ☐ | ☐ |
| Test your learning | ☐ | ☐ | ☐ |
| Keywords | ☐ | ☐ | ☐ |

|  | Excellent | Good | Adequate | Poor |
|---|---|---|---|---|
| Overall opinion of this Course Book | ☐ | ☐ | ☐ | ☐ |

**Do you intend to continue using BPP Products?** ☐ Yes ☐ No

**Please note any further comments and suggestions/errors on the reverse of this page and return it to: Nisar Ahmed, AAT Head of Programme, BPP Learning Media Ltd, FREEPOST, London, W12 8AA.**

**Alternatively, the Head of Programme of this edition can be emailed at: nisarahmed@bpp.com.**

**REVIEW FORM (continued)**

**TELL US WHAT YOU THINK**

**Please note any further comments and suggestions/errors below**